# Teaching College Students
# to Read Analyticall

# Teaching College Students to Read Analytically

## An Individualized Approach

Jan Cooper
Oberlin College

Rick Evans
Texas A&M University

Elizabeth Robertson
University of Iowa

National Council of Teachers of English
1111 Kenyon Road, Urbana, Illinois 61801

Staff Editor: Jane M. Curran

Book Design: Tom Kovacs for TGK Design

NCTE Stock Number 50594

**Library of Congress Cataloging in Publication Data**

Cooper, Jan, 1954–
  Teaching college students to read analytically.

  Bibliography: p.
  1. Reading (Higher education)—Addresses, essays, lectures.  I. Evans, Rick, 1951–    .  II. Robertson, Elizabeth, 1948–    .  III. Title.
  LB2395.C664   1985      428.4'07'11        85-5081
  ISBN 0-8141-5059-4

# Contents

# Acknowledgments

The University of Iowa is widely known for its old and prestigious Creative Writers Workshop, but only a limited number of people are aware that there is another equally vital, well-established tradition in writing at Iowa: the Writing Lab, now over fifty years old and still going strong. For nearly twenty years Lou Kelly, the present director, has been "provoking" (one of her favorite words) students and teachers alike in the Iowa Writing Lab to engage in nothing less than mutually transforming dialogue through writing. It was she who taught the three of us that reading is

> a self-involving experience. Indeed, you are not actually reading unless your mind is interacting with the information and ideas represented on the printed page. As your eyes take in the printed words, as the voice of the writer reaches your ears, you must respond. If you don't, the reading is a boring monologue, just as a conversation is when somebody drones on after everybody else has stopped listening. But when your mind responds to what you're seeing and hearing, reading becomes an exciting dialogue with the writer, an encounter with the voice of another human being. (Lou Kelly, unpublished invitation-to-write, University of Iowa Writing Lab)

As members of Lou's Teaching in a Writing Lab Practicum, we first learned to read our students' writing in this way. It came naturally because that was the way Lou read *our* writing. But this is also the way she describes any good critical reader's encounter with a difficult text. It has become the basis of a series of writing-about-reading invitations given all Iowa Writing Lab students to help them use their full linguistic experience to become more perceptive, analytical readers of the books in their university courses.

We gratefully acknowledge our debt to Lou for both the theory and fundamental approach informing the work we describe here. Surely, one measure of the profound insight she has passed on to us is how we have found her method applicable to diverse circumstances, circumstances that have deepened our understanding of how and why it works. But we are also indebted to Lou for bequeathing to us a sense of respect for the complexity of the task of teaching inexperienced writers, for the thoroughness it takes to understand their individual problems, and for the responsibility entailed to communicate to others the results of what we learn from our teaching. As teachers in the Writing Lab, we are amused that every so often at the start of the fall semester, a new Master of Fine Arts student, an aspiring young poet or novelist just arrived in town to attend the Creative Writers Workshop, wanders into our Writing Lab. Apparently the names *workshop* and *lab* are nearly synonymous to some people. It takes these writers a while to realize they're in the wrong place, which we feel is a tribute to our program.

We are grateful to Keith and Mallory for their cooperation and permission to reproduce samples of their writing, and to the students of Jan Cooper's Introduction to Literature and American Lives classes, all of whom contributed to Chapter 4, whether or not they are directly quoted. We'd also like to thank Richard Lloyd-Jones for reading the manuscript at a critical stage and making useful suggestions.

Jan Cooper
Rick Evans
Elizabeth Robertson

# 1   A Theoretical Context

Jan Cooper

Our introduction to teaching reading came in the University of Iowa Writing Lab, where anyone in the university who wants to improve his or her writing can get individualized instruction. Our school also has a Reading Lab, but in the Writing Lab we sometimes deal with our students' reading skills because so much of what they write elsewhere in the university depends on their ability to comprehend difficult books. Every day, we see freshmen baffled by the essays in their readers or sophomores looking for the "deep hidden meaning" in the "great literature" they've been assigned or even graduate students wading through inscrutable professional articles. Their teachers come to us to ask how persons so lacking in writing "skills" could ever have been promoted from a high school or a freshman composition program or an undergraduate curriculum. We ask these students to write for us after they read a brief, informal statement that assures them we're there to listen to what they *say* in their writing, not to pass out grammar exercises. At this point some of their problems disappear. They don't make as many mechanical errors because they aren't trying to use unfamiliar vocabulary. When they tell us about things they understand well, their writing naturally shapes itself into recognizable forms because they can spare some energy to respond to the rhetorical context. But the minute they return to writing about difficult reading, all the old problems reappear. Their main problem is reading, not writing.

It's not that they can't read at all, although occasionally we see a student who can read very little. When students first come to us, we give them something to read to get them started writing—an "invitation" to help them find an authentic purpose for what they write. Most students have no trouble understanding this reading. But when they turn to longer, more complex discourse that has not been carefully written with them in mind, their understanding of what they are reading falters and their writing immediately suffers as a result.

1

Observing this happen over and over again in the Writing Lab, we have developed certain assumptions and, consequently, certain goals in our teaching of reading, as well as in our teaching of writing.

The following essays describe three applications of what we've learned about teaching reading. In Chapter 2 Elizabeth Robertson recounts her work with a basic writing student who was so inexperienced a reader that even rereading his own writing gave him trouble. In an individualized reading course that carefully balanced familiar and unfamiliar material, this student was able to experience self-involving reading for the first time, as his continuous writing gave him and his teacher a constant medium for exploring his thoughts about what he read. Rick Evans explains in Chapter 3 how he adapted a similar approach in a class of twenty-two freshman English students. By focusing their attention on a single book, Robert M. Pirsig's *Zen and the Art of Motorcycle Maintenance,* rather than assigning readings in a typical freshman anthology, Rick was able to help his students develop their critical reading and analytical writing abilities as he responded to their reactions to the book in their journal writing. Finally, in Chapter 4 I discuss how I have applied the same approach in sophomore literature classes, where my students' writing about reading allowed me to take part in their attempts to understand the assigned texts at every stage of their reading.

## Defining Reading

In working with students on an individual or group basis, we've found that we must begin with a definition of reading that transcends the mere vocabulary recognition or text recall that are the objectives of many reading instruction programs. We do not think of reading as only discrete "skills," in the common use of that word. When politicians call for a return to "basic" reading skills in public school classrooms, they are usually referring to reading speed or superficial word comprehension, aspects of reading that are easy to measure but only a small part of what a good reader does. Instead, if we are to think of reading as a skill, we prefer Michael Polanyi's comparison of skills to "probes" or "tools," instruments through which we extend our "tacit awareness" of the world around us by exploring, testing, and discovering. Polanyi thinks that such a skill literally becomes a part of the person using it, ultimately changing that person, because

> to use language in speech, reading and writing, is to extend our
> bodily equipment and become intelligent human beings. We may
> say that when we learn to use language, or a probe, or a tool, and

thus make ourselves aware of these things as we are of our body, we *interiorize* these things and *make ourselves dwell in them.* Such extensions of ourselves develop new faculties in us; our whole education operates in this way; as each of us interiorizes our cultural heritage, he [or she] grows into a person seeing the world and experiencing life in terms of this outlook.[1]

This is what we think good critical reading is—an experience as real and altering as any other experience. Perhaps it is handier to call it an *ability* rather than a *skill,* since the word *ability* implies the more extensive nature of what it enables a person to do. But we think critical reading is an *acquired* ability that can—and should—be the goal of any class that gives students the opportunity to read.

## Learner-Teacher Dialogues

We have found that we best help our students develop this ability to read by participating in their reading experience through our responses to their writing. As our students begin reading a difficult text, we ask them to "talk on paper" about it as soon as they finish reading. Often they break up what they read into manageable "chunks" and write after each reading session. We call these accumulated writings their "reading journal." We make it clear that in reading the journal we will be looking for their exploration of *ideas,* not for "correctness" of any sort. The journal is their opportunity to tell us what their immediate reactions are—their pleasures, confusions, questions, or disagreements with what they've read. We respond to the journals primarily by asking further questions that encourage students to locate exactly what in the text stimulates their reactions and to identify the wider significances of their observations. Through the journals we try to build dialogues with our students about what they read—"conversations" that have the added benefit of helping us to gauge more accurately our use of class time for our students' needs. We've found that these early exploratory writings about reading usually help students to shape their reactions into more traditional academic forms and encourage even more carefully analyzed responses to reading. But we don't just assign "essay topics" and expect to see finished products. We help students look through their journals to find promising ideas worth pursuing; then we suggest ways in which they can expand their journal entries by providing more documentation from the text and by further considering the implications of their observations. Thus they turn their written dialogues with us about their reading into well-developed papers that would be acceptable to any college teacher.

The beauty of this approach is that it works for students with a wide range of reading abilities—from the most inexperienced entering freshmen to advanced graduate students to the full range of English-as-a-second-language pupils. I have used it in an introductory literature course, a sophomore American Lives class, and even a graduate- and undergraduate-level course, Grammar and Style, in which students had to give concentrated readings of single sentences. We think such an approach could be adapted for any course that requires students to read challenging material.

This approach is flexible enough to accommodate such a range of students because it takes into account fundamental processes of learning that human beings undergo from the moment they are first aware of the world. We think that students accomplish profound learning by integrating new experiences with their store of past events. A person looks through, as George Kelly puts it, "transparent patterns or templates which he [or she] creates and then attempts to fit over the realities of which the world is composed." Kelly calls these patterns, or "ways of constructing the world," *constructs* and observes that a person "seeks to improve his [or her] constructs by increasing his [or her] repertory, by altering them to provide better fits, and by subsuming them with superordinate constructs or systems."[2] Frank Smith says this "theory" that "fills our minds" is "our personal theory of the world, the summary of past experience," and claims it is "the arena of all our thought." Smith feels any sort of comprehension is the answering of questions created by the predictions made according to our past experiences, our "theory of the world."[3]

This process happens at a number of different levels in a person's reading. We recognize letters by categorizing the visual shapes that we have learned to identify as the alphabet. Our understanding of vocabulary depends on previously built semantic classifications and a complex sense of syntactic relationships. Simultaneously, while we're noting these minute details of graphics and grammar, we're also attending to the broad images and concepts we encounter, the various explicit and implicit streams of ideas in a text. Kenneth Goodman's "cue systems" summarize what's involved in this process: in reading, people depend on (1) the recorder strategies they know; (2) their past language experience, knowledge of the structure, intonation, and vocabulary of the language; (3) their general experiential background; and (4) their general conceptual background.[4] No one's memory—short-term or long-term—is sufficient by itself to pull together these many simultaneous awarenesses into the single act we know as reading. It is our constructs, our theory of the world, that enable us to do so much at one time. Actually, we are not doing so very much; we use what we already know to predict and therefore to attend to only the details that are crucial.

Many students, however, have not had sufficient reading experience to develop this ability to select and predict what is most important to retain as they read. By asking them to keep reading journals, we are trying to get students into the habit of looking for connections between what they already know and what they must learn. In Jean Piaget's terms, we create a "need" that results in an "activity" that they gradually "internalize," eventually leading them to further cognitive development. Although Piaget is most concerned with the mental growth of children, he observes that

> From a fundamental point of view, i.e., if we take into consideration the general motives of behavior and thought, there are constant functions common to all ages. At all levels of development, action presupposes a precipitating factor: a physiological, affective, or intellectual need. (In the latter case, the need appears in the guise of a question or problems.) At all levels, intelligence seeks to understand or to explain.[5]

Through our dialogues with students in their reading journals, we attempt to give them just the right question or problem to encourage their intellectual need to explore a text. David Olson and Jerome Bruner have commented that it is

> enormously to Piaget's credit to have insisted and demonstrated that the structure of any ability must be conceptualized in some major part in terms of "internalized activity." Activities one carries out in the physical world . . . come to be internalized or carried out mentally.[6]

This is what we see happening for our students as they continue to write about their reading. They begin to ask themselves the questions we might previously have pointed out. They slowly start to develop the reflective state of mind of a good critical reader.

In order to give our students the chance to explore fully their responses to reading in this way, we have to be willing to adopt several roles at different stages in their reading. We can't just assign a book, conduct a class discussion of the text, and collect essays to be graded. We have to be willing to enter into students' experience of the text at as early a stage as possible. Their writing gives us a marvelous opportunity to do so—but only if we establish ourselves as what James Britton and the London Research Team would call a teacher-as-trusted-adult and invite our students to engage in a learner-teacher dialogue with us about their reading.[7] They must feel free to show us their earliest questions, doubts, confusions, and speculations—what they think of as their "messy" ideas. Only when we're allowed to observe these reactions can we accurately determine how much of their reading they've understood and where the likeliest avenues of further understanding may lie. In such a dialogue, our questions help students more than our judgments or even our authoritative directions for correcting something. Later, as they become increasingly familiar with what they've read, we can become increasingly challenging in our comments. We can engage them in learner-teacher dialogues that do not merely support their first tentative incorporations of what they've read but that also provoke new combinations of ideas and new comparisons with ongoing experiences in their lives. We can encourage them to enter into what Britton et al., would recognize as a "pupil-to-teacher, particular relationship." Eventually a time for evaluation does come, at least in an institution like ours, where final grades are required. But by that time students are ready for an informed judgment of exactly how much they have accomplished.

### Designing Reading Experiences

The three of us have also found that a large part of our responsibility for our students' reading begins before they ever buy their books—it starts as we select what they will read. We find ourselves depending on a couple of related principles when we select materials: We look for reading that will offer our students some immediate opportunity for making connections between their past and their books. But we also look for reading that will carry students beyond their own lives. We agree with Adrienne Rich's observation that

> the college anthology, in general, as nonbook, with its exhaustive and painfully literal notes, directives, questions, and "guides for study," is like a TV showing of a film—cut, chopped up, and interspersed with commercials: a flagrant mutilation by mass technological culture.[8]

We want our students to read *whole* books, to experience the richness and depth of the *whole* journey with a writer, even in a freshman composition class. They need to develop the ability to sustain the process of predicting and comprehending over a lengthy piece of discourse. When our students are very inexperienced readers—those who have somehow made it to college without ever knowing what it feels like to be absorbed in a book—then it's important that there be something in the book that they can recognize. This does not, however, mean that one should assign black students only Afro-American literature or science majors only scientific works or women only writings by women authors. In a perverse mood I began an American literature course with Anne Bradstreet's poetry, expecting to have to work very hard to help my modern Iowan sophomores read through her seventeenth-century spellings and devout religious sentiments. It turned out that I underestimated both my students and Mistress Bradstreet. My students immediately recognized Bradstreet's love of her family and her personal struggles of faith, for they too are members of closely knit large families with strong religious beliefs. They were proud of themselves for being able to appreciate this Puritan poet and as a result were more willing to try to make connections with other writers less like themselves.

It is just this kind of receptiveness to new reading experiences that is one of our major goals for our students. We want them to adopt for their difficult reading what Jerome Bruner calls "the will to learn," which is "an intrinsic motive, one that finds both its source and its reward in its own exercise." The basis for this will to learn, according to Bruner, is a "curiosity, a desire for competence, aspiration to emulate a model, and a deep-sensed commitment to the web of reciprocity."[9] By encouraging our students to get in the habit of looking for connections between themselves and their reading, we gradually help them turn the learner-teacher dialogue into a reader-text dialogue. This involvement with the text can become a valid experience for the student, to be added to the constructs a student already has, to be interpreted and reinterpreted as the student moves on to more analytical writing and, later, as the individual matures.

## Notes

1. Michael Polanyi, *Knowing and Being* (Chicago: University of Chicago Press, 1969), 148.

2. George Kelly, *A Theory of Personality: The Psychology of Personal Constructs* (New York: W. W. Norton, 1963), 8-9.

3. Frank Smith, *Reading* (Cambridge: Cambridge University Press, 1978), 79-87. (This book was reprinted under the title *Reading without Nonsense* by Teachers College Press, 1979.)

4. Kenneth Goodman, "The Psycholinguistic Nature of the Reading Process," in *The Psycholinguistic Nature of the Reading Process* (Detroit: Wayne State University Press, 1968), 25.

5. Jean Piaget, *Six Psychological Studies* (New York: Vintage Books, 1968), 4-5.

6. David R. Olson and Jerome S. Bruner, "Learning through Experience and Learning through Media," in *Media and Symbol: The Forms of Experience, Communication, and Education* (73rd Yearbook of the National Society for the Study of Education, Part I), ed. David R. Olson (Chicago: University of Chicago Press, 1979), 143.

7. James Britton, Tony Burgess, Nancy Martin, Alex McLeod, and Harold Rosen, *The Development of Writing Abilities (11–18)* (London: Macmillan Education, 1975), 67–70.

8. Adrienne Rich, *On Lies, Secrets, and Silence: Selected Prose, 1966–1978* (New York: W. W. Norton, 1979), 57.

9. Jerome S. Bruner, *Toward a Theory of Instruction* (London: Belknap Press, 1966), 127.

# 2 Entering the World of Academic Reading

Elizabeth Robertson

If we define reading as word recognition and good performance on vocabulary and pronunciation drills, then I would not claim that the individual reading course described here necessarily produces "good readers." But if we consider reading as an intellectual activity, a habit of mind, a recognition that there is some relationship between graphic symbols on a page and the thoughts, feelings, ideas, and experiences of real human beings, then I can claim that Keith, the student who took this course, sufficiently overcame his mechanical difficulties with skills and became a real reader.

It seems that we reserve our best teaching efforts for our best readers. They're the ones, we think, who will most appreciate our clever interpretations, our ability to show them relationships among ideas. We want them to have books that will stimulate them, that will connect with other things they know. But for the "basic" reading student, we think that vocabulary workbooks will do the job better than the well-written, thoughtful, provocative prose of engaged minds. We're sure that our basic reading students need skill training. Vocabulary drill. Extensive practice at the sentence level. Reading comprehension cards. They're not ready to read "whole works" yet. The same reasoning makes us think that basic writing students need to study the parts of speech before they can write sentences, practice sentences before they're ready for paragraphs, work with paragraphs before they can write whole essays. We're sure they can't write a connected, fluent piece until we give them the "tools."

This building-block approach to complex cognitive activities only further fragments students' understanding. Students who already have difficulty making connections are forced to attempt to learn reading skills or writing skills in isolation from each other. Their ability—already underdeveloped—to make meaning for themselves out of printed symbols is not exercised at all. Thus it is not surprising that while remedial skills courses often improve students' scores on grammar and usage tests and on reading-for-understanding cards, these students still have great difficulty with their college texts and little success with writing tasks that ask them to analyze and synthesize the material presented in those texts.

## Getting to Know the Student

Keith, the student for whom I eventually developed the reading course described here,[1] came to me very aware of what he perceived as his own inadequacies. Of his reading he wrote:

> I like reading but some time I don't know that I'm am reading. I know I need help in reading and lot of other things. I took reading in high school two years in a row, I improved a little bid but I still need a lot more help. When I read, sometime I say words that are not there.

And of his writing Keith said:

> I have a very nice handwriting, and I like to write but I think I use to many easy words, so I really can't say what I really want to say. When I was home I didn't write or study that much. But now I'm beginning to write and study a lot more.

At the Writing Lab, Keith did indeed begin to write a lot more. In an early writing assignment, he made sure we understood something of his background:

> Coming form a poor background with reading writing and speaking. One of my experience is no one really push me, as I was coming up. Coming from a family of eight people were pretty hard. I could remember some of my brother and sister had to stop go to school and get a job because it were more important too know where your next meal were coming from than go to school. So I'm kind glad other people were interesting in me and took the place's of trying to be a big brother or sister of me. and in a me to go to school everyday. When I got to high school it were impor- tant to learn how to read write and speaking so you can prepares yourself for college. On of my problem was I didn't read enough now I can see how important it was to prepare yourself. Since I've came to the University of Iowa, I'm learning to read, write and speak better.

Here Keith makes us vividly aware of the necessary priorities in his life: "it were more important too know where your next meal were coming from than go to school." But school *has* been important for Keith, and he has been grateful for the interest taken in him. As careful readers and listeners to his writing, we wanted to continue to extend that interest, perhaps even do some of the "pushing" that he missed while he was "coming up." Keith's second paper, a response to an invitation to give us some advice about teaching, tells us more about his background and his school preparation—and it implies a great deal about the teaching he has and has not received:

> I live in a big city and from live in this city all of my life, I have look over everything. In most of the school, I can see that a lot of teachers be glad want 3:00 clock get here more than the student do. I think the princple should look into the school more. Also the student can not learn what the teacher do not teach them. I am not blaming the teacher for what the students do not know, but they can give a little more help. There are some student who do not study, but there are student who can not read or write so its a teachers business to find out a student weakness.

Keith is careful not to place too much blame here on his teachers. But his assessment of the situation is clear: "the student can not learn what the teacher do not teach them."

In *The Study of Nonstandard English*, William Labov has pointed out that

> the principal problem in reading failure is not dialect or grammatical differences but rather a cultural conflict between the vernacular culture and the schoolroom. Progress in reading will depend upon changes in the social structure of the classroom as well as improvement in the technical methods of instruction.[2]

As I read Keith's early writings, I caught glimpses of a world very unfamiliar to me, a world where the value system of the vernacular culture was certainly very strong, but a world that he had kept quite separate from the classroom. I wanted to lessen that cultural conflict, to affirm his experience as valid and as something worth writing about and reflecting upon. Keith became increasingly fluent in the Writing Lab and increasingly able to write about street life as a black in a large city, about what it meant to play football well enough to gain an athletic scholarship to a major university, about growing up in a large family; he became increasingly able to respond to his teacher's questions and come to an understanding of the implications of that experience.

Once Keith became more fluent, we tried to work with him on copyreading—finding the places in his writing that did not conform to standard American English and helping him to correct these variations for audiences that value conformity to the standard. As we copyread typed versions of Keith's writing, I discovered that he could not read his own writing. Or rather, he could pronounce the words, but he could not (or at least did not) read for meaning. In fact, reading for Keith meant simply pronouncing, and he frequently reminded me that he wanted me to stop him and correct him if he pronounced a word wrong. I have other students with the same difficulty and the same misunderstanding. Perhaps they have been corrected so often in grade school when they read orally that they find it difficult to concentrate on anything *but* pronunciation. It's not that they don't know the words. Certainly Keith understood what he had written and could talk about it. But the actual act of reading was so foreign an activity that even his own words had no more *real* meaning to him than those in a published text. The labor of reading left him no energy for understanding.

In an attempt to help Keith become more at ease with the printed word, one of us tape-recorded some chapters from Richard Wright's *Black Boy*. We had Keith listen to the tape and follow along in the book. He loved it. He would come into the Writing Lab, get out the tape cassette and the book, and read. I sat with him briefly several times and noticed that his eyes moved *ahead* of the taped voice, that he was always ready to turn the page. He was learning to look ahead, to "predict" (as Frank Smith would say[3]) some questions about what was coming that he *could* answer. Always before, Keith had strived simply for word accuracy, thinking, as beginning readers often do, that word accuracy is all that reading comprehension requires. Now, for the first time, I saw Keith trying to make *sense* out of what he read rather than just trying to get the words right. Finally he became impatient with the tape because it was too slow. He asked me if it was all right for him to read a story by himself.

A year later, in the spring semester of his sophomore year, Keith was still struggling. He had somehow managed to pass his first-year composition and reading course, mostly by keeping a low profile and because he had a teacher who apparently thought it would be racist not to pass him. He tried so hard, this teacher said, and he was "culturally disadvantaged." But he had failed other courses—not because of his writing, which was far more fluent now, but because he scarcely knew where to begin with his college texts. Even after two semesters of a developmental individualized reading instruction course and the one-semester freshman composition and reading course, Keith tested out at the 6.5 grade level on the Senior Reading for Under-standing Test.[4] I did not consider the test a completely accurate statement about Keith's reading ability. Keith generally had trouble with multiple-choice question formats and needed more time than most students in test situations. Still, his score suggested that his college texts would give him difficulty.

## Developing an Individualized Reading-Writing Course

I decided to see if I could set up a course that would draw on the positive experiences Keith had with *Black Boy* and on his own life experiences, and that would lead him to more fluency when reading his textbooks. Keith *could* read. I knew that. But he also needed to *know* that he could read and that reading was not some impenetrable mystery or merely a mechanical act. The British anthropologist Basil Bernstein, in his study of the social structure of the family and its effect on linguistic development, said that the contexts of learning must make the student feel at home in the educational world.

> We should start knowing that the social experience the child already possesses is valid and significant, and that this social experience should be reflected back to him as being valid and significant. It can only be reflected back to him if it is part of the texture of the learning experience we create.[5]

In our responses to Keith's writing, we had already tried to affirm the significance of his social experience. It seemed equally important to me now that he recognize the place of his own experience in the wider community. It is not merely that others had lived and suffered as he had. He knew he was not alone. But others had *written* about it. Their books were read and respected and were part of the learning that Keith found so foreign.

That Keith was still very ill at ease in the educational world became clear when, in his second-semester freshman course, he was asked to look over the reader he had purchased for the course and then to talk about what was in the reader, what he thought the function of a reader was, and if he liked any of the readers he had used. Despite three semesters of using freshman reader-anthologies, Keith was completely stymied by the term *reader*. He concluded that a college reader must be a person who reads in college and that the function of a reader was to say what he or she had read. The last part of the question (did he like the readers he had used) made no sense at all to him, of course, so he changed it to make sense. He wrote about how college students should *use* their reading to "do okay" in courses. Actually, I rather liked Keith's answer since readers are—after all—people *reading*. But he told me that he knew he was stupid (a word he often used about himself) because the questions really made no sense to him. The difficulty he was having suggested to me not that he was stupid, but that he had been allowed to go through his paces with little idea of what was going on. The stories and essays he'd read in the anthologies had no life or meaning for him and had been connected neither with his own life nor with his understanding or his learning, even at the university. I wanted Keith to learn what reading really could be by having him read longer pieces of discourse that would make sense in his world—at first stories, certainly, but stories that sustained his interest long enough to pull him into a world he could respond to, stories that would touch on his own experience, draw him both into and beyond this experience, and help him reflect on it so that his reading literally became a part of the experience itself.

The book *Black Boy* was a natural, of course, as was *The Revolt of the Black Athlete* by Harry Edwards. Being black and being an athlete on the football team were important parts of Keith's experience and identity. Naturally, I wished to affirm that identity as he tentatively entered an educational world that seemed utterly alien to his own life. I developed the reading list below specifically for Keith, but the list is readily adaptable for students with similar backgrounds:

| | |
|---|---|
| Week 1 | Donald Kaul, "Embarrassment at the Rose Bowl," column in *The Des Moines Register*, 2 January 1982 |
| | Ralph Ellison, "Battle Royal," chapter 1 in *Invisible Man* (New York: Random House, 1952) |
| Week 2 | Harry Edwards, *The Revolt of the Black Athlete* (New York: Free Press, 1970), pp. 8–29 |
| Week 3 | Maya Angelou, *I Know Why the Caged Bird Sings* (New York: Random House, 1970) |
| Week 4 | Angelou, *I Know Why the Caged Bird Sings* |
| Week 5 | Ntozake Shange, *For Colored Girls Who Have Considered Suicide When the Rainbow Is Enuf* (New York: Bantam Books, 1980) |
| Week 6 | John Knowles, *A Separate Peace* (New York: Macmillan, 1960) |
| Week 7 | Knowles, *A Separate Peace* |
| Week 8 | Lewis Thomas, *The Medusa and the Snail: More Notes of a Biology Watcher* (New York: Viking Press, 1979) |
| Week 9 | Richard Wright, *Black Boy: A Record of Childhood and Youth* (1945; reprint, New York: Harper and Row, 1969) |
| Week 10 | Harry Edwards, *The Sociology of Sport* (Homewood, Ill.: Dorsey Press, 1973), chapter 3 |

| Week 11 | Edwards, *The Sociology of Sport,* chapter 7 |
|---|---|
|  | Langston Hughes, "Harlem," available in *Black Voices: An Anthology of Afro-American Literature,* edited by Abraham Chapman (New York: New American Library, 1968) |
|  | Paul Laurence Dunbar, "Sympathy," available in *Black Voices* |
| Week 12 | Gwendolyn Brooks, "We Real Cool" and "The Mother," available in *Black Voices* |
|  | Maya Angelou, "Africa," available in *The Norton Introduction to Literature,* 3d ed. (New York: W. W. Norton, 1981) |
|  | Richard Wright, *Native Son* (1940; reprint, New York: Harper and Row, 1969) (this book was selected by the student) |
| Week 13 | Wright, *Native Son* |
| Week 14 | George Orwell, *Animal Farm* (1946; reprint, New York: New American Library, 1983) |

This list reflects not only some of Keith's interests, but also my desire to expose him to a range of styles. It was important for him to read narratives, but it was equally important for him to encounter the language of his college textbooks in a context familiar to him.

I began with a newspaper column on the Rose Bowl by Donald Kaul because that game was uppermost in our minds that January of 1982. The University of Iowa—which hadn't had a winning football season in twenty years and which hadn't been to the Rose Bowl since 1958—was invited to the Rose Bowl, where it suffered a humiliating 28–0 loss to the University of Washington. Iowans could talk of nothing else, including the sharp-tongued columnist Donald Kaul, who wrote at that time for *The Des Moines Register.* In previous semesters I had Keith read write-ups of different games and watched him eagerly scanning the lines for his own name. Here was the perfect opportunity to have Keith read someone else's opinion about a very important experience in his own life. In response, Keith wrote:

> This man *did* know what he wanted to say to Coach Fry. He told him the way *he* saw the game, but in a straightway. Somewhere in the article, Kaul said he didn't bet on the game—but he sure sounded like he lost some money to me.

Then Keith went on to say how Kaul in his column talked directly to the players. Keith probably missed a lot of Kaul's sharp humor, but he picked up the difference in Kaul's tone to the coach (who, Kaul said, didn't coach well) and to the players (whom Kaul praised).

I had Keith write responses to everything he read—first his own feelings and thoughts about the text, then his response to specific questions. For two of the books, *A Separate Peace* and *The Sociology of Sport,* I helped him develop his short pieces into longer, more coherent statements about the books. I wanted first, though, to engage him in a dialogue with me and with the books. I did not want him to perceive my questions as test questions but rather as an expression of my curiosity about his impression of a book, for sometimes his experience had equipped him to understand a book and to enter into it far better than I could. When he read Ralph Ellison's "Battle Royal," for example, he picked up on the central injustice and irony (though he didn't call it that) of the situation:

> Ellison is recognized as the smartest boy in Greenwood. But him and his friends are treated just like some regular nigger out the streets. Even though Ellison has receive a scholarship, he is still a nigger and he have to pay for everything he recieves.

I decided that we would worry later about the difference between author and narrator. For now I wanted to ask questions that would push Keith beyond his first generalizations about the book. What injustice in particular did he see? How was the character mistreated? What did the narrator's speech have to do with anything? What did he think of the battle royal itself and all those white folks sitting around forcing young black men to scramble for money? Having to write and rewrite and reconsider was hard on Keith. Like most students, he hoped that once a paper was written, it was finished. But he tried to answer my questions and began to use his reading journal as a way of connecting one text with another. A little later, after he had read *The Revolt of the Black Athlete* by Harry Edwards, he reflected on the two works:

> What happen in Battle Royal? It's like what Edwards is talking about. Edwards explains something about Blacks. He said, "first of all, there is no such thing as a free ride. A black athlete pays dearly with his blood, sweat, tears, and with some portion of his manhood." This is the same situation as what happen in Battle Royal.

Keith quoted quite naturally—and aptly—from the text here. He was beginning to recognize that the texts commented on each other, that these were not just isolated "assignments" or "readings." Keith perceived the same essential injustice in Ellison's imaginative recreation of white cruelty to blacks as in Edwards's factual, though impassioned, assessment of the black athlete's position in sports.

Keith delighted in explaining things to me as he discovered that some of his experiences entitled him to "judge" the relevance or the accuracy of a text in a way I could not. *The Revolt of the Black Athlete* certainly spoke directly to Keith's situation—Edwards even mentioned Iowa in his discussion of conditions at college. Keith responded:

> Harry Edwards is saying that back in 1972, black athletes in a predominantly white college don't get a fair chance no matter how good they are. Maybe Edwards is right because he was there and this is the way he saw it. I can't really say that it's that way here at Iowa for me. But some of the things still hold true. For example, he says only a small number of black athletes graduate from college. That's still true here. And another thing Edwards said that holds true here at Iowa—if white guys tear up a lot of things, nothing much happens. But when a black dude sees that, he says to the other black dudes that if we did what these white people do, they will kick us out or make us pay for it.

And Keith went on about professional sports. I noticed here that Keith was able to go back and forth from the text to his own experience, keeping both in mind. I chose *Revolt* because it made such comparisons a possibility. I also selected it because it contains both discussion and narrative, and I needed a bridge book like that to help Keith move from stories to explanatory prose more like the prose of his textbooks. A second book by Harry Edwards, *The Sociology of Sport*, which we read later in the course, picks up on some of the same issues as *Revolt* but uses more technical language, the sort of "textbook" language that Keith was encountering in his other courses. Keith certainly didn't master all of the vocabulary, but he grasped the meaning and was able to comment on the issues. (A year later, when I taught a version of this course to another student, I used a similar pair of books. The first, *Tally's Corner: A Study of Negro Streetcorner Men* by Elliot Liebow, is a lively narrative recreation of the black street-corner culture with some theoretical discussion. William Ryan's *Blaming the Victim* examines some of the same issues of poverty and of family structure. The narrative illustration in *Tally's Corner* makes the more technical, sociological language of *Blaming the Victim* much more accessible. Thus, my student was able to bring a context he already knew from *Tally's Corner* to a text that he first found impenetrable.)

With the fourth work we read, Maya Angelou's *I Know Why the Caged Bird Sings,* Keith was becoming quite comfortable just telling me his reactions and, incidentally, was writing quite a bit more in his first draft because he knew I was not testing him or trying to catch him in some misunderstanding or error. But he also knew that he *had* to read and *had* to write, and that careless reading or unreflective responses would not satisfy the probing questions of his teacher. The selection by Angelou was the first full-length book he read. Later, as the syllabus shows, Keith was reading narratives a little more quickly, but I wanted to give him plenty of time for the first whole book he'd ever read. I also wanted to give him time to react in writing as he went along—again, not primarily as a means of testing his comprehension, though naturally I was interested in that, but as a way of thoroughly engaging him in what he read. He wrote of *Caged Bird*:

> This book seem to be a true story, this is really giving us the real details about how it used to be for Maya Angelou, and many other blacks. The books starts off kind of slow, but as you get deeper in the book it picks up your interest. I don't know if this book is like Edwards or Ellison. One thing I do know is all three story are talking from a personal experience, and how it used to be for blacks. This three story are very good detailed and they make you seem like you are there.

The *truth* of a work seemed to be the thing that impressed Keith most. His use of the word *story* for all three works shows his unfamiliarity with the difference between novel, autobiography, and nonfiction exposition. We came back to those concepts as the course progressed. But I did not want to interfere at first with his dawning awareness that books spoke about true things and things that he knew. Instead, I questioned him about the details; about how, exactly, it used to be for blacks, according to Angelou; about what made it "seem like you are there." Keith's first response to *Caged Bird* went on to say:

> For Maya, life seems to be exciting, important and caring. Maya seems like a very smart girl, and in the story she is trying to learn all she can. Some things she don't understand, but maybe later in the story she will understand. Right now the most important thing to her is her family, not that she don't like living with her grandmother. It's just that she don't know if her mother and father is alive. Another important thing to her is her brother. She love her brother Bailey very much and he is really the only friend and personl family she have. It doesn't really tell you about her personal life in Long Beach, California, but coming from the West and going to the South is a big experience for them. Maybe in California things was different, maybe they had more friends, maybe the people were more richer, maybe there were more things to do, or maybe not. I don't know.

Keith picked up on several things here—Maya's concern for the parents who abandoned her, her love for Bailey, and the impact that the move from the West Coast had on both children. Perhaps even more important were Keith's speculations about things not yet known in the book. He was looking ahead, expecting that Angelou (and the reader) would later come to understand some of the early events in the book and that the reader might later learn something about Maya's life in California. He was asking his own questions about the story and expecting to find some answers as he continued reading.

I anticipated that Keith would have trouble with the fifth work, *For Colored Girls Who Have Considered Suicide When the Rainbow Is Enuf* by Ntozake Shange. I chose it partly because it presented a different aspect of human conflict, not that between black and white but conflict between male and female and between different sets of values. Also, I wanted to see how Keith would react to Shange's decision to write in dialect. Interestingly, the spelling got in his way. Though Keith's own writing and speech tended to incorporate forms considered nonstandard, he was nevertheless disturbed to see unconventional spelling and verb forms in a published text (and he certainly recognized that the forms were unconventional). It gave us another context in which to talk about the copyreading we were doing with Keith's own writing and about the fact that one chooses what language to use depending on what audience is being addressed. Incidentally, Keith realized that he was reading this play much more slowly than he had read the Angelou book, that he was having to read even simple words individually to figure them out. It underscored for him, and for me, that his general reading speed *had* increased and that he was more likely to look for the sense of the work rather than to concentrate on word recognition.

Keith's response to the play was defensive. By then it was important to him that I develop the proper understanding of the worlds we were reading about. He wasn't just answering questions about a piece of fiction—he felt an obligation to interpret for me a situation that I might misconstrue. The play disturbed him and perhaps even angered him. He took it seriously, and in his shocked comment to me that *"all* black men aren't like that," he acknowledged the power and influence that the written word might have. Keith was also able to see and hear the play since I scheduled the reading assignment to coincide with the Public Broadcasting Service presentation of Shange's play.

With *A Separate Peace* by John Knowles, we returned to fictional narrative, and Keith was able to grasp the major story line fairly easily. In his first response to the book, he concentrated on the relationship between Gene and Finny as the most interesting part to him:

> Finny is known as a very good athlete and **Gene** is known as one
> of the smartest boys in the school. The difference between these
> two boys is that Gene likes to study and Finny doesn't. It seems
> like they are kind of jealous of each other because they used to
> have contests of who could jump out of the tree and Finny
> thought he was better than Gene. But Gene knew he was better
> than Finny in the classroom. Finny always found something for
> him and Gene to do to stop Gene from studying all the time.

Since Keith was interested in the relationship between these two young
men, my questions asked him to focus on it more carefully. "How do
you know that Finny is jealous of Gene?" I asked. "Is it just what
Gene says, or are there things Finny does or says that make you think
that?" "If they are as jealous of each other as you say, why are they
such good friends, do you think?" Keith first responded to what
seemed like an impossibility to him: "To me, it doesn't seem like
Gene meant to make Finny fall. *I* wouldn't push or make one of my
friends fall out of a tree just because he's a greater athlete than I am."
It wasn't enough for Keith to tell me what he would have done. I
pushed him to explore the complex relationship between Finny and
Gene, and we went carefully over the sections where Gene discusses
his own confused feelings. Keith had missed some of the subtleties
and the unspoken tensions, but he finally did write more about the
relationship, about Finny's refusal to believe Gene's confession that
he pushed him out of the tree, and about the pressures that can exist
between two athletes. This book wasn't as close to Keith's experience
as some of the others had been—the prep school setting could not
have been more different from his own life. Though he found Gene's
soul-searching somewhat incomprehensible, he was nevertheless able
to make some connection with the human love and jealousy that
governed Gene and Finny's relationship.

*The Medusa and the Snail* by Lewis Thomas was perhaps not the
best choice for Keith. I tried it because I did not want the course to
consist completely of fiction and autobiography. I wanted Keith to
bring to some reading about social science, history, or natural science
the same attention and involvement he was bringing to narratives of
experience. Thomas's essays, I felt, combined some technical language
with very personal formulations of complex scientific concepts. Keith
struggled through about four of the essays and was not sure he
understood them, even when we went over them. The essay titled "On
Cloning a Human Being" captured his attention, though. He had
heard the word *cloning* before, although he was unsure of its meaning.
When he read the explanation of cloning, he was amazed that such a
thing existed:

> Some people think cloning is hard to explain. If I hadn't read
> this book, I wouldn't believe there was such a thing as cloning.
> But as I understand it, cloning is a somatic cell that you can take
> from almost anything to make a new one or another one such as
> plants or frogs. I wouldn't think for plants or frogs this would be
> hard, but for a human being, I would think cloning is very
> difficult. But then again, the way science technology is going,
> almost anything can happen these days.

Once again, I was pleased that Keith recognized in a written text a
source of information and authority. I was pleased that he attempted
to put into his own words a somewhat baffling concept. Later in the
same paper, he expressed his doubts that cloning would work for
human beings. "You would have to clone babies," he said, "because
then you wouldn't have to change the environment." And he pointed
out that Thomas agreed with him: "Lewis Thomas also thought that
if you clone someone you have to clone the whole world. He didn't
think the world is ready for an experiment this size."

By the time we came to Wright's *Black Boy*, Keith was ready to
read through it fairly rapidly. He remembered having read some of
the chapters before and wanted to see how the whole book turned out.
He was quick to find in Richard something of a kindred spirit:

> *Black Boy* is the best book I have ever read. It's about a black boy
> who is very smart and intelligent person. He's not just an ordinary
> black boy. He's kind of different from the other black guys in the
> story. He reminds me of myself in some kind of way. What I
> mean is, it is only so much that a boy can take from some people,
> especially when he didn't know them. I'm kind of like that. I can
> only take so many orders from a person I don't know.

Keith then went on to talk about how Richard coped in the "white
South," how he defied his Uncle Tom, how he would not submit
inside to white folks or black. I was not surprised that Keith identified
himself with Richard. I *was* struck that he wrote about it and talked
about it so willingly, that the formerly shy and silent Keith now spoke
with confidence and even authority of his own feelings in relation to
whites or to anyone he felt had control over him. He had certainly
come to feel much more at home in the academic setting, for he was
finding in published texts validation not only of his experience but of
his reaction and response to that experience. When it came time for
Keith to choose his own book to read, he didn't hesitate. He had seen
a copy of Wright's *Native Son* on my desk and jumped at the chance
to read it. There wasn't quite enough time in the semester for him to
read such a long book, but he finished it in the summer and sought
me out to talk about it.

I had put the poems by Langston Hughes, Paul Laurence Dunbar, Gwendolyn Brooks, and Maya Angelou and *Animal Farm* by George Orwell on the list so that Keith could further extend his range of reading experience. I simply asked him what he could actually *see* in Hughes's poem, and we were able to talk now about images. Then we discussed why Angelou might have taken her title from Dunbar's "Sympathy." *Animal Farm*, of course, demanded that Keith read on more than the literal level. Keith had no difficulty in seeing that the animals stood for human qualities. And though he missed some of the political implications in the book, he recognized the criticism of human society in general. *Animal Farm* allowed us to return to the issue of what is *true* in a book, of how one might have to separate the writer of a book from the characters in it, something that had confused Keith in "Battle Royal."

**The Final Examination**

At the end of the course, I asked Keith to take a final exam, one not unlike the sort he might have to take the following semester in literature courses. Though I had certainly seen plenty of Keith's writing and had worked with him very closely, I nevertheless wanted him to try to bring some of the reading together for himself. All semester I had demanded that Keith be fully present, prepared to discuss the readings twice a week and ready each day with his writing. He could not hide in the back of the room; nor could he decide to let one book slide or to fail one test and forget it. There were always further questions about what he had written. I could tell at once if he had *not* read carefully, and he knew that was not acceptable. Books he had read at the start of the semester came up again and again in our discussions. The final exam represented an opportunity for synthesis. It was another sign from me that I expected Keith to take full responsibility for what he had learned and read. I devised a two-part exam for Keith:

> *Part I*
> Consider the works listed below:
> > *Black Boy*
> > *A Separate Peace*
> > *I Know Why the Caged Bird Sings*
> > *Native Son*
> > "Battle Royal"
>
> Please choose *three* works and talk about how the main character in each tries to be independent.

What kinds of troubles do the characters have?

Why is it so hard for them to "be themselves"?

Who or what gets in their way?

Do you see any similarities among the characters in the three books?

Be as *specific* as you can about each character and about what is happening to him or her.

*Part II*

Please read the following passage. It comes from one of the books you've read.

> It was no longer a question of my believing in God; it was no longer a matter of whether I would steal or lie or murder; it was a single urgent matter of public pride, a matter of how much I had in common with other people. If I refused, it meant that I did not love my mother and no man in that tight little black community had ever been crazy enough to let himself be placed in such a position. My mother pulled my arm and I walked with her to the preacher and shook his hand, a gesture that made me a candidate for baptism. There were more songs and prayers; it lasted until well after midnight. I walked home limp as a rag; I had not felt anything except sullen anger and a crushing sense of shame. Yet I was somehow glad I had got it over with; no barriers now stood between me and the community.

What book is this from?

What is happening here?

What does the character seem to feel? Why?

Keith was nervous about the final. Even though I think he felt fairly confident in the writing about reading he'd done all semester, he still was uncertain of himself in test situations. He did recognize the passage from *Black Boy*, though, and was able to talk about how Richard "thought it was all nonsense," how his family were "pressuring him and making him do something he didn't want to do." And in the "synthesis" question, he managed to explain how the characters in three books (Gene and Finny, Richard, Maya and Bailey) struggled with personal relationships in order to get the things they wanted. I doubt that Keith's answers would have satisfied a literature examiner. In three hours he wrote only five pages. It took him half an hour to read and comprehend the exam itself, possibly because of test anxiety, but also because he still read complex material slowly. The connections he made among the books were more superficial than those he had made in earlier writings and discussion. But I was happy to see this developmental reading student identify, with confidence, a single passage from one of the several books he had read. I was pleased to see him bring together three different texts, using some details and incidents from the texts to support his assertions.

When the course was over, I asked Keith if he would be willing to take the standardized test again. I did not think that it would be an accurate measure of what we had accomplished in the course. We had not so much as looked at a multiple-choice question all semester, and the course had focused on critical reading rather than word comprehension or speed, but I was curious how Keith would do. He achieved a 7.9 score—very low, I thought, until I realized it was nearly a grade and a half higher than he had tested one semester earlier.

Far more important than a test score, though, were Keith's willingness now to pick up a book and his greater need to read for meaning rather than for recognition of single words. I had not sought to simplify reading for Keith—to break it down into simple constituents or simple sentences. I had tried, rather, to match the confusing complexity of his own experience, to confront him with the difficult and demanding task of translating the ideas of others so that he might articulate and clarify *his* theory of the world as he entered into other worlds both like and unlike his own.

### Adapting the Course to Other Students

I have discussed in this chapter a single student in a particular course designed very carefully for him. I have since taught similar courses, one for a group of three students, with different reading lists and different expectations. If I were to describe these courses, I would tell other stories—of Owen, a good reader of narrative who was so unsure of himself that he was utterly unable to read a textbook; of Laura, who could *talk* as though she understood but who had more trouble with the literal meaning of a text than Keith; of Joe. . . . In each case, the students' needs—which I discovered by reading and responding to their writing—governed my choice of books. The students' reading journals were at the center of the course, letting me know what they did or didn't understand, letting me enter into their perception of worlds both familiar and new to them. What has remained constant in each course is my desire to involve students in reading that is meaningful to them, to demand their full intellectual participation in their own education, and to help them find reasons to read beyond the necessity of fulfilling school requirements.

I have often heard teachers of basic reading or writing complain that their work is not stimulating, that they must drudge through dreary exercises and ill-written compositions, never having the opportunity to discuss ideas with their students—or with each other, for that matter. But this course demanded *my* full intellectual participation, as well as Keith's. I read books I had not read before and reread the ones I had, carefully framing specific questions and preparing for what I thought Keith's responses might be. Keith's insights into the books often forced me to reconsider my own interpretations, and I discussed Keith, the books we read, and the ideas we both had with friends and colleagues, just as I discuss my literature courses with them. Keith's perceptions often took me by surprise and challenged me to revise my sometimes too-narrow assumptions, both about a text and about Keith himself as a reader. There was nothing dreary or dull about this encounter with another active mind.

The course may seem expensive—individual, personal. But, in fact, universities and colleges spend a great deal of time and money on individualized instruction in reading labs that use cards and machines to work with students. Special support services and athletic departments hire tutors, desperately hoping that somehow they can explain difficult texts to students who are unable to read the materials for themselves. But a course like this can be accomplished in a reading lab and can even be taught to several students at once in a small class, if the teacher is flexible enough to have comparable but not identical reading lists and if she or he is a sensitive, perceptive reader of student writing. This course is *not* emergency treatment or remedial aid. It is based on the fundamental assumption that real learning takes place only if the student is drawn into the "web of reciprocity" at the deepest level, through engaging the intrinsic will to learn. We cannot afford to squander our best teaching resources on any motive less "basic" than that.

## Notes

1. Rachel Faldet, now of Luther College, Decorah, Iowa, also worked with Keith on his reading, and I am grateful for her many invaluable suggestions about possible readings for Keith and questions to pursue with him.

2. William Labov, *The Study of Nonstandard English* (Urbana, Ill.: National Council of Teachers of English, 1975), 43.

3. Frank Smith, *Reading* (Cambridge: Cambridge University Press, 1978), 83. (This book was reprinted under the title *Reading without Nonsense* by Teachers College Press, 1979.)

4. Science Research Associates: Thelma Guinn Thurstone, 1965.

5. Basil Bernstein, "A Critique of the Concept of 'Compensatory Education,' " in *Education for Democracy*, ed. Rubinstein and Stoneman (Harmondsworth, Eng.: Penguin Books, 1970), 120.

# 3 Response-Ability in Freshman English

Rick Evans

When Sherman Paul, the Carver Professor of English Literature at the University of Iowa, first meets a class of advanced literature students, he asks them to carry on a tradition of responding to reading that reaches as far back as the sixteenth century and commonplace books and that is as native to his American students as Emerson and Thoreau and as recent as poets Charles Olson and Robert Creeley. He asks that they keep a personal journal of their reading. He explains,

> I want students . . . to forego the scholarly-critical mediation of others and to rely instead on their own responses. Response-ability is a responsibility, and it is fulfilled by engaging or encountering a text responsibly. The text is "the jewel center of interest" (Kerouac), the object before one. And reading is an experience.[1]

It was this last sentence, "And reading is an experience," that first led me to consider alternative approaches to teaching reading to my freshmen students in a required second-semester rhetoric course. My earlier attempts to teach reading had been very disappointing. My students had dutifully struggled through a series of drudging assignments in a college anthology and had tediously answered the reading-guide questions at the end of each selection. They were no more involved in each particular reading than they were when they searched for all the presidents' faces in a fast-food "Win a Trip to Hawaii" sweepstakes. If they won, or answered correctly, great! If they lost, well, it was just a dumb game and nobody ever really won anyway. Rarely did my students become excited about what a writer had said, or share with me or the class some personal insight, or even care enough to ask their own questions. Reading for them had become only a routine of scanning and then selecting the necessary information for passing a test.

I wanted instead to teach reading as an experience, one that, like many others in my students' lives, might engage them, maybe even change them. My assumption was that if I were able to offer such an experience to them, not only would they enjoy reading and therefore read more, but the analytical abilities they needed as "college-level" readers would grow. And since the reading that I had required of students in the past had not encouraged their involvement or realized those abilities, I needed to try something new. I asked the freshman program coordinator if I might be allowed for a single semester to alter the standard pedagogy, and my request was granted.

## Focusing on One Narrative

About six weeks into a sixteen-week term, I introduced my students to a sequence of journal writing about reading, specifically writing in response to *Zen and the Art of Motorcycle Maintenance: An Inquiry into Values* by Robert M. Pirsig. I chose this book for several reasons. It's a story, the narrative of a trip from Minneapolis to San Francisco Bay. Whenever I ask students to recall their favorite book or their most memorable reading experience, they never fail to mention a story and to explain that they had identified with a particular character, that the details of place and time so involved them that they felt they were there, and that this certain story helped them realize things about themselves they had never quite understood before. I wanted my students to be engaged in these ways. *Zen* is also a book full of Chautauquas, "popular talks intended to edify and entertain, improve the mind and bring culture and enlightenment to the ears and thoughts of the hearer."[2] Most of the reading these students would be doing the next three years of their college career would be of a similar kind—historical essays that chronicle the causes of the American Revolution or the results of the Russian Revolution, chapters in a biology textbook that describe natural phenomena and offer formulaic explanations for their occurrence, even studies in psychology that speculate why people under stress tend to respond the way they do. The Chautauquas in *Zen* do not offer any sort of content-specific preparation for all the college reading that students may encounter. However, *Zen* does involve readers in a wide variety of ideas and different levels of abstraction comparable to those in other courses. Finally, *Zen* is an extended piece. It demands that readers use their analytical abilities to sustain the cognitive processes of constructing and integrating both a personal (in their journals) and a communal (in class discussion) understanding of their work. The edited selections of college anthologies make no such demands.

I asked my students to keep a reading journal, making two entries of three pages or more twice a week, which allowed me as a reader and as a teacher to share in those cognitive processes I was encouraging. In my initial invitation to them I said,

> When I ask you to read *Zen* I am asking that you have an experience. I am asking that you ride across the country with Robert Pirsig, that you see the red-winged blackbirds in South Dakota, that you climb a mountain in Montana, that you cruise a freeway in California wine country. I am also asking that you consider what Pirsig says, that you risk thinking and feeling as he thinks and feels, or maybe the greater risk, that you think and feel differently.

I cautioned them not to tell me just what happened in the book, or to write a book report, unless they were so confused in their reading that retelling the story to me and to themselves would help clear it up. I wanted them simply to talk to me on paper about their thoughts and feelings as they were reading the book. I promised them that I would respond in writing to one of their two entries each week. Then, if they wanted, they could respond to my responses the following week.

There are several practical reasons underlying this schedule of entries and responses. I felt that only one entry a week would not keep their attention focused on the book long enough to engage them fully in the cognitive processes I was hoping for. More than two entries, however, would overwhelm me. I decided upon the three-page length of each entry for similar reasons. (Some students from the beginning handed in entries up to six pages long.) I chose to respond at least once a week because if students did become involved in the reading, they would need some form of feedback—if nothing else, my acknowledgment of what they'd told me. Yet I didn't want them to adopt me as the arbiter of those thoughts. One response was enough to guide but not determine their thinking. Finally, I offered them the opportunity to "talk back" to me with one of the following week's entries. I wanted to give them the chance to rethink and further develop their ideas as well as to experience writing about reading as a sharing dialogue between themselves and a teacher.

Many of the students were confused at first and asked, "Is there a *particular way* you want these *papers* written?" or "What do *you* think I should write about?" or even "How are you going to *know* if I read the book?" These questions impressed upon me again how limited their understanding of reading and writing about reading really was. Reading, at least in school, had been a "task" to perform under the examining eye of a teacher. Then once they tried to "say what the teacher wanted them to say the way the teacher wanted them to say it," they were judged, defined as either a "good" reader and writer or a "bad" reader and writer. But now I was changing the experience, and its newness was threatening.

### Focusing on One Student

One of my students, Mallory, a second-semester freshman on a tennis scholarship, was particularly reluctant to begin her journal. We had two or three conferences in my office trying to figure out the problem. It was clear to me that she was reading *Zen* and had several things to say about it. Each time she left my office, she promised that tomorrow, "for sure," I would receive her first entry. Tomorrow always came, but not Mallory's entry. Finally, after nearly three weeks, I told her how worried I was becoming. If she waited much longer she would be hopelessly behind. In her first entry the next day she wrote in response to Pirsig's discussion of technology:

> Whenever I find myself getting stuffy about how technology has made our world so plastic . . . I make myself think of exactly how terrible it must be to be cold . . . all winter with no relief. . . . It's easy to glorify the early days when men and women "tamed the wilderness" . . . like in all the books and movies. But we never know the sufferings of these people. . . . I think Pirsig has the answer for me—its okay to reject some of the things that technology brings about and try to get along without it, but I still have to appreciate it and relate to it. . . .

Mallory, still thinking of me as her examiner and anticipating how she expected me to respond, wrote at the end of this first entry:

> There's good thought in this, but you get quite a-ways from the book—you seem to ramble a lot, just restating the same ideas. I'd like to have a more concrete idea of what you think about the book. You seem to be really interested in the ideas you [covered]. . . . They could be polished up some if you want to write further on the subjects.

I liken this first entry to the "talk" James Britton et al. refer to in *The Development of Writing Abilities (11–18)*:

> It is probable that of all the things teachers are now doing to make their pupils' approach to writing more stimulating, and the writing itself seem a more integral part of the manifold activities of the classroom, it is the encouragement of different kinds of talk which is the commonest and most productive factor. Talk is more expressive . . . talk relies on an immediate link with listeners. . . .

> [and these] exchanges of conversation allow many things to go on
> at once—exploration, clarification, shared interpretation, insight
> into differences of opinion, illustration and anecdote, explanation
> by gesture, expression of doubt; and if something is not clear you
> can go on until it is. Whether or not the mind is partly engaged
> in thinking about what may be written later, there's a good chance
> that the incubation . . . of the writing is given a boost, by the
> widening of the consciousness if by nothing else.[3]

Britton et al. are here referring to classroom talk and its importance as
a way of permitting students to try out their thoughts before they
begin to write. I hoped that by extending this notion of classroom
talk to talking on paper in a journal, I would encourage a similar
kind of exploratory reading.

Mallory's first entry was a bit shallow and, as she herself pointed
out, rambling, but what she had done was not wrong. Just the
opposite—it was exactly right. In these journal entries I hoped that
Mallory, along with all my students, would "talk" to me as they read
*Zen*. At the same time, I encouraged them, through my comments, to
understand reading as an involving experience, an authentic and
personal experience like any other. Quoting her own editorial remark,
I wrote back to Mallory:

> There *is* "good thought in this," Mallory, and you stay quite close
> to the book. In fact, without the book you probably wouldn't
> have writen about the ideas you did.

I showed Mallory just what I was referring to when I borrowed her
phrase "good thought" in the excerpt about technology. I bracketed
her talk about technology, and in the adjoining margin I asked her
some very specific questions about what she had to say:

> What are some of the things technology makes available to you
> that you have decided to do without?
> Why have you decided to do without them?
> Also, what things can you appreciate or relate to? And why?

With these questions I was trying to lead her from the kind of talking
apparent in her first journal entry toward a more detailed and
developed consideration of her concerns. I was trying to show her
where she, as a reader, might be better able to think about what Pirsig
said by more fully understanding her own thoughts about technology.
At the same time, I wanted her to see where she, as a writer, could
expand what she had said to give more specific information about her
own experience with technology. I think it is important to note here
that I was neither trying to get Mallory to go back to Pirsig's
Chautauqua on technology and do a careful analytical reading, nor to

expand this particular journal entry into careful, analytical writing. I was simply showing her what indeed represented "good thought" and suggesting how she might further develop it.

Mallory did not choose to respond directly to my questions, but she began to do what I had asked with other topics current in her reading of *Zen* (and with regularity, I might add). In a later journal entry, for example, she struggled to distinguish Pirsig's notion of "quality" from something he calls "good." She wrote,

> I think I'm a quality tennis player, but I don't consider myself a good player. I have too many shortcomings. My quality comes in that I'm quick, I have good racket control, good touch, and have a very wide range of shot selection. I can hit almost any kind of spin. I think most of these characteristics would constitute criteria for a quality player. However, I honestly don't think I'm a good player. My mental game isn't tough enough. I do really dumb things sometimes (like get real mad). I don't use the assets that make me a quality player.
>
> On the other hand, I don't think Chris Evert-Lloyd is a quality player, but she's definitely good. She doesn't have a well-rounded game, she can only play one style, and there are several kinds of shots she can't hit effectively. But she's a good player . . . unbeatable most of the time. . . . I guess I'm really referring to performance with these examples. It doesn't seem that the level of performance—which is what people usually go by in deciding whether or not something is good—has necessarily to coincide with . . . quality. . . .

Here Mallory is accomplishing more than "talking" about ideas. She is using references focused on the details of her own experience to understand Pirsig's highly abstract concepts. In this excerpt she successfully distinguishes the ideas of "quality" and "good" by first bringing her experience to her reading of Pirsig, articulating and exploring how that experience suggests quality and good differ, and finally introducing an abstract notion of her own, that of performance, to represent their difference. Clearly Mallory does not fully understand this concept of performance that she has introduced. Yet I could see her cognitive processes of constructing Pirsig's ideas for herself and integrating those ideas with her own experiences. In my response to this journal entry I was careful to draw her attention to this excerpt— explaining to her how it was certainly acceptable discourse and how, with some editing, it could become a perceptive, well-crafted essay. I suggested she might tell me more about her notion of performance and how it helped her distinguish between quality and good. I did not respond with questions because none were necessary. This excerpt was essentially a completed piece.

At this point Mallory was not just "talking," exploring her thoughts by simply speaking them. She was moving from impulsive thinking to reflective thought. James Moffett describes it best:

> The primary dimension of growth seems to be a movement from the center of the self outward. Or perhaps it is more accurate to say that the self enlarges, assimilating the world to itself and accommodating itself to the world. . . .[4]

As a reader, Mallory was extending herself beyond the text in her struggle to assimilate and integrate the new concepts she was receiving with those concepts she already possessed. Journal writing provided her with both the dialogic context for that extension as well as the opportunity to see and become aware of the analytical reading, writing, and thinking that she was doing.

What Mallory had not yet accomplished as a writer was a single, whole, controlled piece of analytical discourse. And if I continue to assume that Mallory's journal writing was suggestive of her reading abilities, then neither had she, as a reader, completely "thought through" some aspects of her reading of *Zen.* Up to this time, after seven weeks of reading and journal writing, virtually all my responses to Mallory, as to all my students, were attempts to show her what she was doing. But not one of my students experienced a nice, neat, linear progression of their reading or writing abilities. They were not consistently writing carefully shaped, analytical pieces in later entries. There are several reasons why this occurred; one was that their writing reflected how involved they were with their reading of *Zen* during that particular week. Because of this, I felt it was important that Mallory and the others attempt to pull together what they had been shown and now show me what they had learned. Moffett suggests that the

> control of behavior [in this case, the expression of their reading and writing abilities] becomes possible only as awareness of these abstractions arises. In short, increased *consciousness* of abstracting has as much to do with developmental growth as has progression up the abstraction ladder. I believe that growth along one dimension fosters growth along the other.[5]

I wanted to see how aware they were, how conscious they were of their own abilities, and if indeed they could focus those abilities upon the production of a complete reading and controlled expression of that reading.

At the beginning of the eighth week I gave a new invitation to my students:

> Earlier this semester when I asked you to read *Zen*, I asked that you have an experience. I hope that you have had several and that those experiences have been both vital and personal. In this invitation to write I want you to tell me, show me, one experience in particular. . . . I hope that you will use an idea that Pirsig explores, or an experience that Pirsig has, or a scene that Pirsig offers to illustrate your own experience for me.

I was asking my students to demonstrate how much "response-ability," as Sherman Paul calls it, they had gained in their reading of *Zen*—if they had indeed met the text "openly, ready and willing to be changed by it, to come to know it for what it is and respond to it."[6] Mallory began her final piece by telling me of her meeting with *Zen*, what she had finally come to know of it, and how she responded to it:

> When I began reading *Zen*, I remember being kind of freaked-out that I was so much like John and Sylvia. I knew right away that I was a romantic in Pirsig's view because I often feel "alienated from the whole rationalized structure of civilized life, looking for a solution outside that structure, but finding none that are really satisfactory for long." I really enjoy thinking, but I don't like numbers and facts much. . . . I steer clear of chemistry and math . . . they clutter my mind, but I get into art and literature because they represent freedom and creativity to me, as they did to John and Sylvia.

Going on, she observed:

> Before reading *Zen* I was aware of . . . "left-brain" and "right-brain" people. . . . However I never realized that this split was as profound as Pirsig makes it. . . . its the artists vs. the scientists . . . but as I apply it to my world its also the "believers" vs. the "analyzers" . . . the "easy-going" vs. the "regimented". . . . There have been several times now that I have been able to say . . . "Hey this situation . . . can be defined in Pirsig's theory of the romantic/classic split." The most recent event [like this] occurred when I decided to take a personality test.

Mallory's personal response to her meeting with *Zen* was apparent in the picture she painted of herself, using the details of *Zen* as her paint. She, like John and Sylvia, was a "romantic." (Notice how well Mallory interpolated a quotation from the book into her sentence—no mean accomplishment.) She went on to suggest what being a romantic meant to her—a left-brained believer, an easy-going artist. How much she had come to know *Zen* for what it is and responded to it is clear in her articulation of that romantic/classic split, as well as the extension through application of that split into her own world. She further extended her understanding as she continued:

> On a recent trip, one of the girls, Kemi, pulled out a personality test that she was supposed to be taking. I like these tests because I learn about myself. . . . [But] even with the first few questions, I could see it dividing people into those with spontaneous, feeling personalities or those with more exacting, factual ones—that is, romantics and classics. By Pirsig's idea of the division between classics and romantics, nearly all the questions had only two answers, implying that I was either one type or the other—with no middle ground. . . . I was aware of this "underlying form" of the test that illustrated Pirsig's romantic/classic theory right away. . . .

The understanding of "response-ability" that Paul suggests focuses mainly on what readers bring to their comprehension of a text, yet in Mallory's writing I saw evidence of another kind of response-ability developed through reading and journal writing—the kind that encourages readers and writers to use what they have learned to respond to the world around them. If Mallory had not understood what she had read, if she had not been able to talk or write through that understanding, she would not have been able to extend and include in that understanding the "underlying form" of this personality test. Not only was I sure that Mallory was using the reading abilities—responsiveness, perception, analysis—that I hoped she as reader would develop, but she was using similar abilities as a writer and, maybe most significant, as a thinker engaged in understanding the world around her.

There is still, however, a higher awareness for which all the reading, writing, and thinking become a means, still another kind of response-ability. Paul claims that in reading and journal writing,

> not only does one, finally, discover a voice and a form congenial to one's intimate way of thinking, one discovers in persistent themes (image, ideas, concerns) one's very self.[7]

Mallory seemed to discover this in her writing. She concluded her paper:

> In both [*Zen* and the test] . . . however, an attempt is made to bridge the gap between the two types. . . . The formulations of the test did offer a unifying solution. They go through a process of explaining how certain traits of the two types allow each other to compliment the other. . . . Hence the test formulators and Pirsig come together on another important point. Pirsig also goes through a long process—his search for quality. . . . He proposes that it is quality that binds the opposing types, classics and romantics. . . . He also goes on to say that it takes some kind of system of values to determine quality. . . . This is where *Zen* and the test coincide. They both recognize that in order for the conflicting types . . . to be reconciled, they must have something in common that they both appreciate—values. . . . I believe [we] have

> a tendency toward good things. We value goodness and seek it wherever it is. With this as a value, we will have to cross the line between the two types in order to get the best of both worlds. We may still be predominantly one type or the other, but we will share the traits [so that we] have complete and balanced personalities.

There can be little doubt that Mallory had discovered, in her writing about the persistent themes of *Zen*, if not her "very self," then at least those particular values that for now support her understanding of the world. Mallory realized that both romantic and classic "types" are searching for good in the world, and if in that search they share what is good in themselves—their quality—they may indeed complement one another. They may be able to help themselves and others "have complete and balanced personalities." As a person, I was gratified to hear another person express such values. As a teacher of reading, I was impressed with the degree to which Mallory's reading of *Zen* had affected her awareness of herself and the immediacy with which she had heard and responded to what Pirsig had to say.

**Assessing the Success of the Course**

Mallory's development of her own "response-abilities" was typical of the class. Still, this pedagogy failed some students. A few were never able to read or write for themselves. They were always trying to perform. A few dutifully reported in their entries *only* what was happening in the book. Those same few persistently asked if they were responding in the "right" ways or not. Interestingly, they would often ask me this without having read my comments in their journals. And it was those same few who would, in class discussion, demand that I divulge what *Zen* was *really* about: tell the secret and the hidden meaning. They were unwilling to accept, in spite of several conferences, that to be a response-able reader, they had to be responsible for working toward their own understanding. If those few students had risked responding with their own thoughts and feelings, as I had asked in the opening invitation, they would have stopped performing and begun to discover, in the voice and in the expressive form apparent in their journals, their own intimate way of thinking. They would have been able to tell themselves the secret and the hidden meaning of *Zen*.

More numerous were those students who were unable to think about Pirsig's Chautauquas and the concepts he presented there as ably as Mallory had. Their journal entries focused chiefly on the narrative of the book. One student in particular wrote a very interesting final paper analyzing Pirsig's relationship with his son, Chris, and how that relationship was similar to and different from her own relationship with her father. Initially I was disappointed that these students had not written more about the Chautauqaus. Then I realized that the ideas and relations of ideas that they did recognize were just as complicated and involved the same reading, writing, and thinking abilities as did the Chautauquas.

Even given these problems, the students for the most part realized the goals I had set for them. Their reading of *Zen* had hardly been a routine of scanning and selecting the necessary information for a test. Often during class discussions they asked me about Pirsig—did I know him, had these things really happened, and where was he now. Several students complained that they had to read and then reread everything. When I questioned them about why they were rereading so much (since I had said nothing about rereading), they answered that they really didn't mind; besides, they needed to if they were going to understand a "thinker" like Pirsig. The clearest indication, however, of their involvement with *Zen* was how much of themselves they brought to their journal entries. Like Mallory when she used her experience as a tennis player in her struggle to distinguish Pirsig's idea of "good" and "quality," another student told of her experience as part of the McDonald's restaurant chain to support Pirsig's notion of a system. And another argued with Pirsig, claiming that grades were a necessary part of education. She used as evidence her own experience as a student in both graded and ungraded courses.

Whether or not my students developed the perceptive abilities that college-level reading demands is something that, after all, is very difficult to determine in any quantitative way. Discrete skills can and should be tested so that students with particular problems can be identified and helped. However, teachers and students of reading often confuse being able to read, something that tests can discover, with being an able reader, something that we still know very little about and therefore cannot test reliably.

In my approach to teaching reading, I assumed that my students were able to read, but that they needed help becoming able readers. I selected a particular kind of book and asked that they respond to that book in a particular way. My window, as it were, into their development was the reading journal. The responses, perceptions, and analyses presented there allowed me to follow and guide their development as readers and writers. The final paper I asked students to write was an invitation to tell me, to show me, what they had learned generally and specifically about reading and writing. Mallory's response again, I think, is typical of most of the students. About what she learned generally she said:

> I see all these ideas of Pirsig's as being pretty fundamental although as he says, its often the most obvious ideas that we are most blind to. I think they are ideas that I was gradually formulating on my own, but I don't know that I would ever have gotten them as refined as they are now. . . . they have helped shape my perspective and the new ideas I encounter in the future will be filtered through this perspective and I will determine where they fit, or if they do fit, within my own special view of life.

She then commented on what she had learned about reading:

> I now appreciate reading more. . . . I know now that I have to involve myself in the reading, apply it to myself, for it to be helpful. Lots of times now while reading my psychology I'll stop and try to see how it is that I utilize the theories they put forth—if I really interact the way they say I do. . . . Before I thought of texts as just coming from some computer or something, but now I can feel the authors in the books and I look for times that some type of personality shows through.

Finally, in response to what she had learned as a writer, she wrote:

> I think the biggest change of all is the way I see writing now. I enjoyed writing in high school . . . [it] was very planned, almost regimented—outlines, a certain structure, punctuation, grammar, vocabulary. I still believe in these a lot. . . . But now that I look at it—this mustn't be writing at all—its learning to plug my ideas into someone else's formula. This must be why I've gotten into the journals so much. Its great to let my mind go and write it all down. . . . I feel free to write until I'm talked out on a subject—I don't have to follow a set outline, and you're right about writing helping someone to think through a subject. . . . I think my writing has improved too. . . . At the very beginning when I wrote those first papers [in the course], I can see that I was writing generalizations. . . . Then, as we got into *Zen*, I started using the book as a springboard for my ideas. I gave my opinion, but was careful to give evidence for it. . . . I know I've learned tons in this class. It has really been an experience for me. Unlike other classes where I'm fed information, I feel like I actually grew in this class.

As a teacher, I actually grew in this class too. I found my approach to teaching reading very demanding. Mallory's journal was approximately sixty pages long—the range of journal lengths for the class was from forty-five to nearly seventy-five pages. The time I spent reading was substantial. Yet I noticed that as the semester progressed, the students needed less and less direction from me—brief responses and suggestions were all they really needed or wanted. After all, most of them felt very good about presenting what they had to say the way they wanted to say it. With other classes I often felt as if I were "correcting," even though I have never given grades as responses to particular invitations to write. In this class my experience changed completely. I became involved in the students' journals in the same way they were involved with *Zen*. The journals became for me a significant learning experience, and my responses were those of a truly engaged and interested reader.

One course does not magically create an able reader, and I certainly want to make no such claim for the course I've just described. Yet, one course can, I think, get students started in a direction that is, potentially at least, more productive than others. Beyond my course, I hope that my students were eventually able to condense the responding process, which extended over eight weeks in our class, and apply it in their other classes. I hope that they were able to develop the kind of flexibility needed to read a novel or sociology experiment or biology textbook and still continue to bring themselves and their experiences to their reading. I hope that as they developed as readers and writers, they developed as thinkers too. And, finally, I hope that all of them were able, as was Mallory, to take pride in their "own special view of life."

## Notes

1. Sherman Paul, "Journals: The Dialogue between Text and Self," *Iowa English Bulletin* 30 (Spring 1981): 6.

2. Robert M. Pirsig, *Zen and the Art of Motorcycle Maintenance: An Inquiry into Values* (New York: Bantam, 1974), 7.

3. James Britton, Tony Burgess, Nancy Martin, Alex McLeod, and Harold Rosen, *The Development of Writing Abilities (11-18)* (London: Macmillan Education, 1975), 29–30.

4. James Moffett, *Teaching the Universe of Discourse* (Boston: Houghton Mifflin, 1968), 59.

5. Moffett, p. 24.

6. Paul, p. 6.

7. Paul, p. 6.

# 4   Reading Literature Analytically

Jan Cooper

College literature teachers usually think that the least they can expect their students to be able to do on the first day of class is *read*. What we often don't realize is just how different and how cognitively more complicated the reading of literature is. To appreciate literature fully, students must become closer readers than they've ever been before—on the one hand more minutely sensitive to the beauty of language masterfully used, but at the same time more broadly conscious of the cultural traditions and historical circumstances in which any work of art dwells. The task is so complex that it makes many students feel like they're learning to read all over again, no matter what their reading backgrounds are. We're not just teaching them what there is to know about a specific work or a particular author; we're also teaching them a way of looking at the text, a process of thinking about it. In the fullest sense of the term, we are reading teachers.

At some point most of us ask our students to write about what they read, but the traditional role that student writing has played in college literature classes is small. Most teachers assign a few limited, formal papers or essay questions on exams and respond only through their evaluation of the finished writing. Perhaps we too need to learn more about reading, about how to bring to our students' writing some of the patience and open-ended inquisitiveness we habitually use when we read our literary texts. We need to examine our students' writing periodically, since their writing can give us a more thorough understanding of how well they are reading.

I asked students in two literature courses to write to me extensively before, while, and after they read assigned texts. Because any liberal arts sophomore at the University of Iowa can choose literature courses to fulfill general education requirements, I knew I might find quite a range of reading abilities among my students. In our Writing Lab I had known one student who, despite passing both freshman courses, still had read so little that he believed we were giving him a new book when we traded a paperback version of the novel he was reading for the hardbound library copy he'd been using. For this young man, a text was simply a material object, something he couldn't imagine being replicated in different sizes or typefaces. He was, of course, an extreme case. Far more common are the numerous students I've met who may know that a book can come in different covers but who have so little awareness of literary forms that they call anything in print a "story," be it poetry, essays, drama, or novel. This blurring of terms indicates, I suspect, a serious lack of reading experience and may be the source of their confusion about such literary techniques as persona or irony or even their unwitting plagiarism when they're asked to write critical reports using secondary materials. On the other hand, I have also seen students who read as much Shakespeare in high school as most undergraduate English majors study in college, but who were convinced by some well-intentioned Gradgrind that there is one and only one "right way" to appreciate "great works of art." These students are often expert plot summarizers but are reluctant to think beyond the safest literal meaning of a text. Any or all of these sorts of readers can typically be found in the two courses I taught, an introductory literature class in which students read poetry, drama, and fiction, and an American Lives course that covered American biographical and autobiographical works.

**The Reading Survey**

To find out exactly what combinations of these and other levels of reading experience my students had, I began each course with a reading survey. I tried to make the survey a natural continuation of introductions on the first day of class. After checking the roll and inviting everyone to tell the group a little about themselves, I told the class that I wished I could talk to each of them individually about their reading backgrounds so that I could use what they already knew or did not know about literature in my plans for the course. But since there wasn't time to hold so many conferences before I drew up a schedule, I wanted them instead to spend a half hour or so of that first class meeting telling me on paper about their previous experience with books. I listed some questions on the board to get students thinking about literature:

> What previous experience with literature have you had? Did you study it in high school? What novels or plays or poetry or short stories did you read then, if any?

> Have you ever read anything that made a great impression on you? If so, what was it? Why do you think it appealed to you so? What do you think "literature" is? What, if anything, do you think makes it different from other kinds of writing?

I tried to emphasize in this request that I wanted to read what the students had to say, that I needed this information in planning the reading selections. I also tried to make clear that I was not going to read this writing with a red pen poised to circle every mechanical error. In the short time they had to write, it would be difficult for almost anyone to write perfectly correct prose. Instead, what mattered to me was how much they could tell me about their backgrounds, the titles and names of authors they could remember, and the attitudes toward reading they could recall.

By emphasizing my interest in what the students had to say, I was trying to encourage them to think of me as an audience with whom they had a common interest, not as an adversary who was only looking for mistakes. As a writing teacher, I knew that students usually write better, using more detail and less stilted language and making fewer mechanical errors, when they are saying something important to a person who is genuinely interested in what they have to say. They do their worst writing for a reader they think of as merely an examiner, someone who already knows the answers and reads only to correct. From the start, I wanted my students to know that I would take what they said seriously. By doing so, I hoped to give them a chance to write as well as they possibly could and to begin the honest dialogue with me about their reading that would continue in all the other writing they would do in the course.

Some teachers would call this first-day request a "diagnostic" writing. It's true that when I spotted someone who could not write more than three or four lines in half an hour or whose writing had many consistent errors, I wanted to see more of their writing quickly to decide if they needed extra help in the Writing Lab. But "diagnosing" these problems was not the primary reason for the survey. Its main purpose was indeed to "survey" my classes—to get the "lay of the land" and learn my students' past experience with literature—so that I could make better plans for the two courses.

I was so anxious for this information that I found myself stealing minutes away from my other work to glance through these surveys right after I'd collected them. As I read, suddenly the vague mass of faces became studded with individual personalities—the student who vividly recalled following Jean Valjean through the sewers of Paris, the student who was once declared dyslexic, the several who had hated the poetry they had to read in high school but who also confessed to scribbling verses from time to time themselves. After scanning the stack, I went back and considered the surveys more slowly, pausing to write comments, almost always questions, in the margins. "What was it about that book that 'grabbed' you?" "What were you reading in tenth grade that made you realize that 'a book could be as much fun as a basketball'?" At the end of each person's survey I wrote a brief closing comment, thanking each writer for what they'd told me. I wanted to show them from the beginning that I really read what they wrote so they'd be more willing to "talk" to me when they began writing their reading journals.

## The Reading Journals

After reading the surveys, I made up a syllabus to hand out on the second day of class. I had already chosen the entries on the reading list so that books could be ordered beforehand, but I was able to make last-minute adjustments in the scheduling of topics and in the order- ing of our class discussions on the basis of what students wrote in the surveys. I spent most of the second class period explaining the schedule and how students were to write about each reading assignment in their reading journals. These journals provided a means for each student to discuss her or his reading with me individually. Like the surveys, these were not intended to be polished products but, rather, exploratory writing in which they told me what questions they had, what they liked or disliked, or what had stood out for them in what they had read. If they ran across unfamiliar words or references, the journal was the place to ask me about such things. If they thought of questions they'd like their classmates to discuss, they could make suggestions in the journal. If the reading was so difficult for them to understand that just figuring out what happened was a major task, then they could tell me in the journal what they'd deciphered and why it had been so difficult. But I made it clear that these journals were meant to be more than mere plot summaries. As a Writing Lab teacher, I'd seen students dash off a single empty paragraph for other teachers' journal assignments, and I wanted my students to understand that I expected more of them. I would plan discussions around what they wrote to me in their journals, so they needed to tell me as much as they could. In order to have a little time to look over their journals and make plans, I asked students to turn in these writings at least a day before the class discussed the reading, and I taped an envelope on my office door for this purpose. I told them I might read portions of someone's journal as a way of starting discussion and asked them to inform me if they had written something they wished to keep private.

The first reading journal entries handed in by both classes were much the same—too short and general. I had to comment on them carefully and turn them back for revision. Some of the introductory literature students' reactions to their first assigned poem provide a good sample of their early journal-writing problems. I had asked them to read Marianne Moore's "Poetry" because it recognizes the resistance that many people feel toward poetry, a resistance that we almost always find in introductory literature courses. Sherri's response to the poem was typical:

> As a rule I hate poetry; but after reading this poem a second time I have to admit I agree with what is being said. I especially like the expression: "the same thing can be said for all of us, that we do not admire what we cannot understand." This is true for me.

This was Sherri's entire response to the poem—only three sentences. But in those sentences she had expressed a definite opinion and singled out the line that evoked it, the beginning of analysis. To challenge her to explain the significance of the line that caught her attention, I wrote right after her response the question "How exactly is this true for you—what's another example of a time you haven't admired something because you didn't understand it?" Another student, Janet, had a similar reaction to the poem:

> I especially liked this poem because I myself do not really like poetry. I think it is kind of useless. This poem was very understandable, though, unlike some of the other pieces I have read.
>
> The one part of the poem that I really liked was when it said "the same thing can be said for all of us, that we do not admire what we can't understand." I think that really has meaning. I think that is true because people do not admire things they don't understand because they don't know what to admire about it.
>
> I thought the whole poem had real underlying meaning even though it may not be apparent until you read it several times.

Janet had written a longer entry than Sherri but still hardly said much, so I tried to encourage her to explore the implications of her statement by recalling a personal experience. "What's an example of this that you've seen in 'real life'?" I asked in the margin of her paper, hoping that when she compared Moore's abstract statement to a particular event she'd have more to say. The response of a third student, Rusty, demonstrated a different sort of problem, also typical. All he had to say about his reading was

I think it is about Poetry, why else name it "Poetry".
I can't figure it out, but what I know about poetry you can fill a
thimble.

The length of his response indicated to me that he probably wasn't
trying very hard to understand what he'd read, but his final derogatory
remark about himself also gave me a hint as to why he gave up so
easily. He was telling me that he didn't think himself capable of
reading "Poetry" and that he wasn't ready even to try. I tried to let
him know I was there to help him start by asking simply, "What
exactly do you not understand in the poem? Where do you first start
getting lost and why?"

When I handed back the first journals the next day, I told the
students in each class that I knew this was unfamiliar writing for
most of them, that they were probably used to teachers who only
wanted finished papers that were very focused and correct. Instead, I
was asking them to let me in on their reading process much earlier,
when they were thinking, I hoped, about many ideas, some of which
they might later decide were wrong. But just because my request was
less formal than most teachers' didn't mean that I wanted them to
take it casually. They could tell me anything in their journals as long
as they thoroughly showed me where they got their ideas. In what
words of the poem, lines of the play, or pages of the novel did they
find the ideas they were thinking about? What had they seen of the
world that made them notice those things? The more carefully  they
could trace what they had gotten out of their reading, the better they
could show me what we needed to talk about in class. But just telling
them what to do didn't immediately produce the entries I wanted. We
had to go through the process of questioning and response several
times before the majority of the class understood what I wanted.

Most of my comments on these first journal entries were very
specific questions placed in the margins to show my students exactly
where they could tell me more. Sometimes my questions asked them
to tell me more about themselves, or were designed to encourage them
to make comparisons between what they already knew and what they
had read so that they could judge the reading more critically. "Why
do you find Bradstreet's expression of sorrow over death so realistic?"
I asked one young man and promptly received an account of how he
felt when a close friend died of cancer. It was not hard for him to turn
that early narrative into an expanded analysis of Bradstreet's religious
questioning later in the course. Other times my comments asked for
more documentation. "What lines or words in the poem confused
you?" I might ask when someone pleaded total ignorance. Or if they

tossed off an airy generalization, I might write something like "What did the grandmother in 'A Good Man Is Hard to Find' do that made you think she was hypocritical in the end?" Sometimes I asked for the why of a situation, as in "Why does the last line of Hughes's poem sound so different to you? Does it make you go back and read the rest of the poem any differently?" On the first journal writings I usually wrote at least three or four substantial questions in the margins to show students several places where they could tell me more. Once the students had a clearer idea of just how specific they could be without "boring" me, they needed fewer comments. As the course progressed, I usually wrote only one or two questions that suggested a new way of looking at something they'd written about, such as, "Do you see any similarities in the way Franklin talks about keeping account of his moral life and his business transactions?"

## In-Class Writing

Occasionally, the journal entries would tell me that almost everyone in the class was having trouble reading a book. At such times I found in-class writing useful. Thoreau's *Walden* is a good example. Most of the students in my American Lives class dutifully tried to wade through its early chapters, noting in their journals each word they didn't understand or each reference that baffled them, until most of them bogged down in disgust for this "selfish hermit." To help them reach a better understanding of Thoreau, I began class by handing out a paper listing the following questions:

> Do you have a Walden?
> Think of a place in nature that you like to go to,
>          a place you've been to many times,
>                   in different seasons,
>                   at different times of the day.
> Describe it for us, let us *see* the place as you do.
>      Do you visit it alone or are you always with someone?
>      What exactly do you look at—look for—each time?
>      Why do you keep returning?
>      How has it changed in your eyes over the years?
> What, if anything, has this place taught you over time?

I asked students to think about these questions for a while and then to write about them in class for half an hour or so. Because the class period was seventy-five minutes long, we had time to read a few of the responses aloud. As the students read their writings and questioned each other, I gradually began asking them to compare the places they'd described to what Thoreau said about Walden Pond. By the time I got the second batch of journal writings on *Walden,* most of the students were beginning to appreciate Thoreau's ideas more. In fact, a few of these in-class writings were such well-conceived starts that I encouraged the writers to develop their comparisons in more-finished papers.

## More-Finished Papers

It seemed to me that exploratory writing took my students only half as far into critical reading as I had hoped. Expressive writing like a journal entry or answering a question in class helps a reader develop the habit of reflection, of pausing to consider different points of view, of connecting what an author has said to what the reader already knows of the world. But a reader can learn even more, once that groundwork is laid, by going back over a text to focus on a single idea and to document it thoroughly, presenting it in a form and tone that is pleasing for another reader to follow. The demands of syntax itself force a student writing about reading to see new juxtapositions of detail. When we craft sentences that will say what we mean with a minimum of ambiguity and when we start rereading our sentences through the eyes of others, we see new combinations, more profound hierarchies of thought working in a text.

When I asked for the more-finished papers, I was *not* asking for "writing with a thesis," the old I-jump-through-the-hoop-you-pat-me-on-the-head five-paragraph theme, the keyhole essay, the *explication de texte.* I called these papers "more-finished" rather than "finished" because I've found that not even good writing is ever as completely finished as the prefab formulas lead students to believe. There is always more to say and a better way to say it. The main goal should be gaining a more refined understanding of what one is talking about, rather than plugging information into a superficially neat pattern of canned ideas.

In the more-finished papers I wanted to give my students the chance to develop ideas that had already come up in the other writing they'd done for me. I wanted them to take one idea as far as it would go, not trim or inflate something to fit a predetermined mold. My only structural demands were that the more-finished papers be focused, well documented, and as stylistically refined as possible. These writings could evolve into whatever shape their writer found appropriate, as long as I was allowed to participate in the process from the beginning.

I handed out the following description of typical stages for a more-finished paper to provide guidelines for the process I wanted my students to follow:

Stages for More-Finished Papers

1. Look through your reading journal and find the idea most worth pursuing. Discuss it with me.

2. Write about the idea, telling me all the thoughts, questions, and possible support you've found for it in your reading. Make this a continuous piece of writing (not just a page of notes or a list of points), and skip every other line to leave me room to make comments. Turn in this draft and I'll return it to you, probably with questions that will lead you to gather more material and develop the idea further.

3. Shape the idea by working out the most effective arrangement of points. Outlining may be helpful now. Skip every other line in this draft too; then turn it in to me so that I can make stylistic suggestions.

4. Shape the language by cutting out empty phrases and pseudo-academic terms, substituting specific and concrete words for less informative ones. Read the draft aloud to yourself to see if you are writing in a natural "voice." This draft should also be written on every other line when it is turned in to me, so that I can mark it for copyreading errors.

5. Make a final draft by recopying in ink or by typing; this time you may single-space. Reread your paper several times to make sure the "mechanics" (spelling, punctuation) are as correct as you can make them.

In the introductory literature class I asked my students to write at least three more-finished papers, one about each of the kinds of writing we studied (poetry, drama, and fiction), and in the American Lives class I asked for two papers. I found that students had to write at least two of these papers to benefit adequately from the process of shaping that I was asking them to go through.

The papers that resulted from this refining process were the culmination of one development in the course—the students' increasingly analytical reading. The reading surveys and early reading journals had suggested to me that most of my students were superficial readers. They read the words on the page, kept track of plots, noticed outstanding detail in character or setting, but did not read closely enough to examine subtleties of motivation or structure or diction. As they wrote more about what they read, they began to realize that there was more to write about. When I challenged them to be more detailed and speculative, they had to pay more attention to what they read. The focusing and documenting requirements of the more-finished papers extended this analytical process, making students look even more closely at a text. But analysis—the careful examination of parts, the zeroing-in on a particular angle of a subject—is only one half of critical thinking. To appreciate fully what one is reading, one must also be able to synthesize. I tried to encourage this process of thinking in another kind of writing: generalizing papers.

## Generalizing Papers

These writings came at the end of a large amount of other work, when we had either finished a unit of similar readings or come to the end of the semester. They too were a culmination of previous writings. As the term progressed, many students naturally began comparing what they'd read, talking about common themes or devices they'd seen in several works. And so it seemed appropriate to stop and ask them to attempt to answer the larger questions of literary study, questions that have no clear-cut answers, even for the experts, but that nevertheless give a reader a deeper appreciation of what an author has accomplished.

For example, at the end of the introductory literature class I decided that a discussion of each of the genres we had studied might be useful. I began by making the following in-class writing assignment:

> What Is Fiction?
>
> To get us started discussing this topic at our next class meeting, I'd like you to begin by writing about it in class today. You have the whole hour, but I don't expect you to compose a completely finished, definitive answer. Instead, I'd like to read your accumulated thoughts now that you've had almost a semester of studying fiction off and on.
>
> Consider these questions and answer all or any combination of them as thoroughly as you can, using specific examples from the short stories and novels we've read:
>
> What is a short story? What is a novel?
>
> What can be done in a short story that can't be done in a novel? What can be done in a novel that can't be done in a short story?
>
> Which do you enjoy reading more? Why?
>
> What is fiction? What can be done in fiction that can't be done in a play or a poem?
>
> Of all the fiction we've read, which did you enjoy the most? Why?
>
> Warning: It's better to answer one of the above questions thoroughly than to simply dismiss each of them one at a time with a vague sentence or two.

We carried on our consideration of this and similar writings about poetry and drama by discussing them in class, but we might as easily have continued them in more-finished papers. We arrived at no sweeping theoretical consensus, but this comparative approach to discussing form encouraged the students to look at the structural elements of their reading in a broader perspective. The American Lives class had an even more obvious opportunity for synthesis because the question "What is an American life?" had been recurring in class discussion all semester. After students read about the American experience of different generations and ethnic backgrounds, such a question gave them a chance to tie together all they'd read with all they'd observed of America in their own lives. As a result of that writing, an especially revealing discussion erupted in the last class meeting when an Iranian exile finally asked the question he'd been wanting to put to his classmates all semester: "How long will it take you to accept us as part of this country?" Because they had read Frederick Douglass and Black Elk, Thoreau and Maxine Hong Kingston, the other members of the class were better prepared to explain to him the treatment any outsider receives in our culture. Despite the many kinds of people comprising American society, they told him, we've always mistrusted someone who was noticeably different from the majority. As the class asked their Iranian friend about similar acts of discrimination in Iran, the whole group came to the conclusion that a mistrust of diversity was a human, not only an American, characteristic.

## The Teacher's Role

Asking for these five kinds of writing—reading surveys, reading journals, in-class writing, more-finished papers, and generalizing writing—means asking for a lot of work. Much of it had to be commented on and returned immediately, so as not to delay a student's progress on a paper. It was rarely as orderly as it may sound, but it wasn't as difficult as some may fear. Much of my response to the reading surveys and in-class writings occurred in my oral remarks to the class rather than in writing on the papers. Often a number of students would mention in their journals the same questions or confusions about a reading assignment, thus giving me the basis for class discussion and making it unnecessary to write individual answers on each journal entry. Sometimes I arranged for my students to read their in-class writings or journals to each other in small groups, where their classmates responded with suggestions and constructive criticism.

This was also a helpful activity when the students were in the early stages of the more-finished papers. By the time they reached the later stages of those writings, I knew their papers so well and was reading for such selective purposes that these papers were not as hard to respond to as the finished papers many teachers receive from their students at the end of the semester.

The journals were, however, the most time-consuming task for both my students and me. In each class I had to cancel journal entries a week before a more-finished paper was due. The rest of the time I think we all depended heavily on the journals to help us gather our thoughts about a reading assignment before class, even though all of us complained about them from time to time. I found commenting on the journals most strenuous early in the semester, when I wanted to establish myself as the right kind of audience and when the students were struggling to understand what I expected of them. As they wrote more, however, many of them began to anticipate my comments. Talking more to themselves than to me, they were answering their own questions, challenging their own assumptions, and catching their own misunderstandings. This made my commenting easier, but, more important, these students were beginning to develop for themselves the habit of reflection, which was the main goal of the journals.

I have noticed that there are two operating principles that make commenting on any kind of student writing more effective and less time-consuming. They are, simply, to be honest and to ask questions. When a teacher gets to know her or his students as well as such frequent writing allows, it is sometimes tempting to forget that the only authentically supportive remark is a true one. Students can sense false praise, and even if they choose to believe the deception, they are hurt more by a falsely positive statement than by no comment at all. In the long run, an accurate sense of their abilities serves them better than the temporary ego building of "strokes." Being honest, though, need not mean being tactless. Marginal spasms of sarcasm may reassure a teacher of her or his own intelligence, but it rarely teaches a student much. If a student says something that genuinely impresses me, I underline it and briefly try to explain why I was struck by it. I usually ignore redundancies and overly general remarks in the journals and in-class writings, or I challenge them with questions. Some writers get themselves going by stating the obvious or using filler material to keep their pens moving while they're writing their way to their next thought. When students' writing includes flashes of insight, I comment on the thoughtful ideas and pass over the rest.

But when vague generalities or repetitions of obvious facts seem to be all a student can say, I try to stimulate the student to think more deeply by asking questions. Nothing does as much good as a well-placed, specifically worded question. Questions are one of the best ways to convince students that their teacher-reader is an interested audience rather than a bored examiner. Questions have an almost magical generative power. They can pull things out of us that we never knew we had. If, for example, I write only "support needed" on a student's paper, not only am I failing to give this student any idea of what I expect as support, but I am also failing to give him or her any sense that I'd genuinely like to know exactly what in the reading led to the statement that needs backing up. If, however, I pick up a student's own wording and write, "What exactly does Franklin say that makes you suspect his altruism was 'just so he would look better to society and thus get farther and farther ahead'?" I can indicate exactly what kind of support is called for, and also let the student know I am reading and thinking about his or her ideas carefully and am willing to read more. Or, in a similar way, if a student supports an assertion with a quotation but does not sufficiently tie it to the argument, I would be more inclined to ask, "Which of the words that Othello uses in this quote give you the feeling he's losing the ability to think calmly?" rather than make the dead-end remark, "Explain quotation more," because it would point out exactly what I, the attentive reader, needed to know to be convinced completely.

Questions are invitations, not judgments. If they're worded properly, they suggest a new way of thinking about something but allow the possibility of other equally interesting perspectives. Like a good invitation, they try to attract a voluntary commitment; they do not order. But, just as when a person receives too many invitations, too many questions can pull a writer in too many directions. Covering a paper with comments of any kind usually confuses a student. I've found that sometimes I have to read a student's writing several times to decide which points might be most effective at encouraging re-thinking. Then I try to ask the writer only two or three of the most important questions, usually questions that lead the student to the most analytical paths.

The time and the energy it takes to find such questions are, it seems to me, well spent. Through this manner of "talking" with each individual, I felt I learned much more about how well every student was understanding the reading. I didn't need to spend time on activities like reading quizzes, which might assure me students had read the material but which would tell me little more. I didn't waste energy trying to devise "topics" for papers that might or might not turn out to be fruitful questions for a majority of the class to answer. Through my comments on their reading journals and the drafts of their more-finished papers, I was able to focus their attention on "critical" matters—places where they might indeed engage in literary criticism but also the places where they were identifying concerns in the reading most critical to them personally.

When students read critically, they internalize the experiences of the author or the characters they read about, extending their cognitive framework to absorb their book's view of the world. When students write, they externalize their experience to fit the frameworks of others. Both processes require similar abilities, similar analysis and synthesis, comparing and contrasting, connecting and reevaluating, the same weighing and judging of ideas. The more students use reading and writing together, the more they will learn from both activities.

# A Selective Bibliography

For a fuller view of the range of reading research and theory, we recommend *Linguistics, Psycholinguistics, and the Teaching of Reading: An Annotated Bibliography*, compiled by Yetta M. Goodman and Kenneth S. Goodman (Newark, Del.: International Reading Association, 1971) as an especially sage guide to shorter articles in the field of reading published before 1971. For teachers interested in further exploring the philosophical and psychological theory behind our particular approach, we suggest the following:

Britton, James. *Language and Learning.* Harmondsworth, Eng.: Penguin Books, 1970.

> By tracing the cognitive development evident in the ways children acquire and use language, Britton fully discusses the theory that language is a means of organizing a representation of the world. Chapters 4 and 5 directly address practical applications of this theory in primary and secondary school classes and also strongly suggest its implications for language teachers at other levels. This book is particularly useful when read in conjunction with Britton's *The Development of Writing Abilities (11–18)*.

Britton, James, Tony Burgess, Nancy Martin, Alex McLeod, and Harold Rosen. *The Development of Writing Abilities (11–18)*. London: Macmillan Education, 1975.

> A text of central importance for teachers of writing and reading, this study describes the stages of writing development that Britton and his colleagues saw emerging in the 2,122 student texts they collected from teachers all over England. In seeking ways of classifying that took into account the nature of the tasks represented and the demands they made on the writers, the researchers discovered that traditional categories (narrative, description, exposition, and argument) were inadequate to provide a full conceptual framework for the writing process. The explanation of the "functional categories" that resulted from this

study—expressive, transactional, poetic—has come to form the basis for understanding writing as a process and for understanding how the writer's sense of audience affects the success of a piece of writing.

Bruner, Jerome S. *Toward a Theory of Instruction.* New York: W. W. Norton, 1968.

In language that is more direct and systematic than his equally thought-provoking *On Knowing: Essays for the Left Hand,* Bruner describes a dynamic model of intellectual growth, discussing particularly well how language learning assists in that development. Teachers of any subject should find his discussion of the features of a sound theory of instruction thorough and useful.

Clark, Eve H., and Herbert H. Clark. *Psychology and Language: An Introduction to Psycholinguistics.* New York: Harcourt Brace Jovanovich, 1977.

Taking as their central assumption the idea that language is primarily communicative, Clark and Clark present both theory and research illustrating the most widely accepted psycholinguistic understandings of language comprehension (listening), language production (speech), language acquisition, and the relation of meaning in language to human thought. Teachers of reading will find this book useful for the detailed picture it gives of all the psycholinguistic processes naturally developing in students as they learn to read.

Fulwiler, Toby, and Art Young, eds. *Language Connections: Writing and Reading across the Curriculum.* Urbana, Ill.: National Council of Teachers of English, 1982.

The essays in this collection seek to explain the relationship between writing and *real* learning (as opposed to rote learning), but the three essays on reading especially stress the importance of the experience and expectations that readers bring to a text. Ann Falke's "What Every Educator Should Know about Reading Research" is useful to teachers looking for background information on reading research, and both Falke's essay and Elizabeth Flynn's "Reconciling Readers and Texts" are noteworthy because they are based on the psycholinguistic model of reading developed by Frank Smith and Kenneth Goodman.

Gibson, Eleanor J., and Harry Levin. *The Psychology of Reading.* Cambridge, Mass.: MIT Press, 1975.

Gibson and Levin's approach to understanding reading is inter-active, suggesting that neither "top-down" models (such as those of Goodman or Smith) nor "bottom-up" models (as in Ruben-stein or Gough) accurately describe reading processes. Instead, in the view of these authors, reading is an "adaptive process," the active and flexible response of a reader to both the demands of a text and his or her own purposes. Gibson and Levin's survey of reading research is extensive, although they certainly have an information-processing emphasis.

Guthrie, John T. *Comprehension and Teaching: Research Reviews.* Newark, Del.: International Reading Association, 1981.

Each essay in this collection explains a current point of view of an important issue in reading research. The first six essays present contributions that psychological and sociological theor-ists have made to the understanding of reading processes, while the second six discuss what educational researchers have found out about instructional practice. Guthrie clearly identifies major concerns in these two areas and, perhaps unwittingly, does an equally good job of suggesting the communication gap that exists between the two areas of research and the major concerns within each area.

Kelly, Lou. "One-on-One, Iowa City Style: Fifty Years of Individual-ized Writing Instruction." *Writing Center Journal* 1 (Fall–Winter 1980): 4–9.

This article presents a brief history of the University of Iowa Writing Lab and a full description of how writing is taught there, explaining how—and why—instruction in the Writing Lab evolved from the "attitude sentence outline" to its present form on the student text as the center of a learner-teacher dialogue. Because writing about difficult reading is a major component of the UI Writing Lab instruction, this article has important implications for teachers who want to try an individ-ualized approach to teaching reading as well as writing.

Kelly, Lou. "Writing as Learning for Basic Writing Teachers and Their Students." *Basic Writing Journal* 3, no. 4 (Spring–Summer 1984): 38–54.

Drawing on learning and psycholinguistic theory, Kelly explains the assumptions behind the training of basic writing teachers and the teaching of writing at the University of Iowa Writing Lab. She illustrates the move from expressive writing to academic discourse that underlies instruction of both basic writing students struggling with their first college texts and upper-level or graduate students who may be too well trained in academic or pseudoacademic prose to engage in the exploratory, generative writing that helps them learn to read critically.

Labov, William. *The Study of Nonstandard English*. Urbana, Ill.: National Council of Teachers of English, 1975.

In language accessible to the nonspecialist, Labov briefly presents some sociolinguistic principles that help define the relationships between nonstandard and standard English. He speaks specifically of "reading failure" and discusses what reading teachers can learn about nonstandard usage that will help them work more effectively with their students.

Martin, Nancy, Pat D'Arcy, Bryan Newton, and Robert Parker. *Writing and Learning across the Curriculum 11–16*. Montclair, N.J.: Boynton/Cook, 1976.

This study examines the practical implications of theory introduced in Britton's *The Development of Writing Abilities (11–18)* and looks at the role language plays in learning in all parts of the curriculum. It is written specifically for elementary school teachers but has far-reaching implications for reading and writing instruction at any level. It discusses ways that can be used to help any student see school reading and writing as valid, engaging activities by using student writing as "reading texts" and by choosing other texts that are related to students' own experiences.

Moffett, James. *Teaching the Universe of Discourse*. Boston: Houghton Mifflin, 1968.

In this seminal work, Moffett describes the pedagogical theory of discourse that underlies his "naturalistic" language curriculum, a curriculum based on the notion that students become proficient in writing not by analyzing it but by using it in as many "real" rhetorical situations as possible. Moffett sets up his "spectrum of discourse" not in traditional modes (narrative, description, persuasion) but according to a hierarchy of levels of abstraction, beginning with interior and socialized speech (dialogue, drama) and then moving to reporting (narrative), generalizing about what has happened (essay), and theorizing and arguing about what might happen. Such a theory of discourse has implications for teaching reading as well as writing: it influences the choice and progression of texts to be read and suggests the sort of written or oral responses that are most realistic for teachers to expect from students at different times in a course.

Piaget, Jean. *Six Psychological Studies.* Translated by Anita Tenzer; translation edited by David Elkin. New York: Vintage Books, 1968.

The six essays in this volume provide an introductory summary of Piaget's theories of the mental growth of children and the relationship between human biological processes and the acquisition of knowledge in general. Although not intended as a prescription for pedagogy, this work does suggest, in its frequent contrasting of child and adult thought, exactly what the goal of an individual's education should be.

Polanyi, Michael. *Knowing and Being: Essays by Michael Polanyi.* Edited by Majorie Grene. Chicago: University of Chicago Press, 1969.

Polanyi discusses his theory of knowledge, drawing on his background as a physical chemist to demonstrate the element of personal judgment that is as crucial to knowing in the sciences as it is in the humanities. Of particular interest to teachers of reading are the essays in Part Three, in which Polanyi most clearly explains how "tacit knowing" contributes to development of any complex skill.

Smith, Frank. *Reading.* Cambridge: Cambridge University Press, 1978. (Reprinted under the title *Reading without Nonsense* by Teachers College Press, 1979.)

Smith's approach to understanding reading has a "top-down" emphasis suggesting that the nonvisual information supplied by readers is more important than the visual information supplied by texts. According to Smith, children learn to read and eventually become fluent readers simply by reading, and he argues that they will only read if reading, like any form of learning, makes sense to them or answers their questions. This fundamental understanding of how good reading abilities are developed should not be confined to elementary teachers; reading teachers at any level will find it applies to their students.

Smith, Frank. *Understanding Reading: A Psycholinguistic Analysis of Reading and Learning to Read.* 3d ed. New York: Holt, Rinehart and Winston, 1982.

This book is a carefully presented introduction to research in a variety of disciplines—psycholinguistics, communication and learning theory, the physiology of the eye and brain interaction— all of which inform Smith's speculative model of the "fluent reading" done by a skilled reader. Smith's theoretical analysis of the reading process is both accessible to new students of reading and stimulating for the specialist.